The Peter Collins Speedway Book

The authors wish to acknowledge the photographers whose work illustrates this book, namely WRIGHT WOOD (*Speedway Mail*), MIKE PATRICK and TREVOR MEEKS (*Speedway Star*), BRIAN SCOTT (*Sunday Express*), RAY COOPER, MICHAEL GILBERT, KEITH LAWSON and GEORGE HARTLEY.

The Peter Collins Speedway Book

Edited by Richard Bott

Stanley Paul London

Stanley Paul & Co Ltd
3 Fitzroy Square, London W1P 6JD

An imprint of the Hutchinson Publishing Group

London Melbourne Sydney Auckland
Wellington Johannesburg and agencies
throughout the world

First published 1977

Set in Monotype Baskerville

Printed in Great Britain by litho at The Anchor Press
Ltd and bound by Wm Brendon & Son Ltd
both of Tiptree, Essex

ISBN 0 09 129400 2

Contents

Introduction

HELLO! I'm Peter Collins and I want you to know what a thrill it is for me to have my own Speedway book; almost as big a thrill as winning the World Championship in Poland last September.

That was the greatest day of my life, the fulfilment of a dream. Okay, you may think it is silly to talk about a life's ambition when I will be only twenty-three years old this year. But I dreamed of winning that title from my tenth birthday.

1976 was an unforgettable year for me. Two months after my triumph in Katowice I said goodbye to my bachelor days by marrying my fiancée Angela Hilton and we moved into the house of our dreams. I never imagined such success and happiness when I was a sixteen-year-old apprentice fitter. I certainly never imagined myself as an author, though most of the credit for this book must go to my Business Manager Richard Bott, *Sunday Express* sports writer and editor of the *Champions Book of Speedway* series.

Dick has been looking after my business interests for nearly four years and has helped me to obtain various sponsorships which provide me with the very best racing equipment. I would like to take this opportunity of saying a very big thank you to those sponsors for having the confidence to support me.

Since I won the World Championship I have signed some very lucrative contracts and it is good to know that so many firms are prepared to put money

A typical action shot of World Champion Peter Collins.

Castrol

F.C. BRUGGE
Congratulations, Peter Collins
Mirror Sport
COLLINS THE WORLD ACE
Daily Mirror
Daily Mail
Collins is king
Now Collins cracks the cash barrier

into Speedway as well as other more widely publicized sports.

Speedway as a whole benefited from my success because the sport received a tremendous amount of extra publicity in the newspapers and on television. If this encourages more sponsors and a greater number of riders benefit, my efforts will have been doubly worthwhile.

I hope you enjoy my book. And when you have read it I hope you will know a lot more about me as a person as well as a Speedway rider. For those of you who were disappointed that Angela and I turned our wedding into such a private affair, I hope the exclusive pictures from our wedding album will compensate. You can also see us in our new home.

But, basically, my book is about Speedway and I have tried to include something to interest you whoever you support. Enjoy your sport.

PETER COLLINS

I first saw Peter Collins in action at Belle Vue in April 1971. It was Ivan Mauger who brought him to my attention. As a Speedway journalist, I invariably used to spend the second half of a meeting in the pits, talking to riders, hunting for newsworthy items.

On this occasion, Ivan, who was then World Champion, said: 'Come and have a look at this boy Peter Collins in the novices race. He is going to be something special.' I followed Ivan to a vantage point by the pits gate and saw the seventeen-year-old Collins deftly picking his way through the field with uncanny control for such a raw youngster.

'See what I mean?' said Ivan. I did. From then on I hardly missed an opportunity to see young Collins in action. Later that season, when he was riding for Rochdale Hornets in the British League's Second Division, I recall a meeting at Bradford. The Odsal track was an awkward shape and many experienced riders could not handle it. But Collins, who had never seen the place before, rode so expertly that he had the Yorkshire fans buzzing with excitement and admiration. He was a 'natural'.

Basically, he was, and still is, a quiet, easy-going young man. No airs and graces. I offered to be his manager a few years ago because I thought he would be very easily exploited if the 'sharks' got hold of him. I am happy to say that we have a good working relationship and have become good friends, too.

After editing the *Champions Book of Speedway* for seven years, to which Peter was a regular contributor, I felt the time had come to launch a *Peter Collins Speedway Book*. I have retained the records section from the *Champions* Book for those of you who like your statistics kept up to date.

As a sports writer I am aware of the value of 'hard news' and I think you will find that Peter makes some quite startling revelations. The success of this book is virtually guaranteed by Peter's wonderful World Championship win. Its future as an annual depends largely on his continued success as a rider. But those of you who have thrilled to his track exploits must feel as confident as I do that here is a 'super star' who will be with us for a long time.

RICHARD BOTT

Sunday Express sports writer Richard Bott at work on the *Peter Collins Speedway Book*.

Potted biography

FULL NAME: Peter Spencer Collins.
DATE OF BIRTH: 24 March 1954.
BIRTHPLACE: Urmston, Manchester.
NOW LIVES AT: Lymm, Cheshire.
WIFE'S NAME: Angela.
WEDDING DAY: 20 November 1976.
FAMILY: Eldest of six. Four brothers (Leslie 18, Philip 16, Neil 15, Stephen 10) and a sister (Ann 20).
COLOUR OF HAIR: Brown.
COLOUR OF EYES: Blue.
HEIGHT: 5 ft 7 in.
WEIGHT: 10 stone.
SCHOOLS: Partington County Primary, Oaklea County Junior and Broad Oak County Secondary.
JOB PRIOR TO SPEEDWAY: Apprentice fitter.
FIRST INTEREST IN SPEEDWAY: 1962. Parents took me to Belle Vue when I was eight.
FIRST INTEREST IN MOTOR CYCLES: About the same time. Rode around the fields on old cut-down road machines.
SPEEDWAY DEBUT: 1970 in second-half at Crewe.
LEAGUE DEBUT: 1971 for Rochdale Hornets in British League Division Two. Debut for Belle Vue in Division One same season.
FIRST-SEASON FORM REPORT: Averaged 9.80 for Rochdale (30 meetings) and 6.36 for Belle Vue (11 meetings). Made international debut for Young England *v.* Young Czechoslovakia. Finished fourth in Second Division Riders' Championship.
FIRST MAJOR HONOUR: British Junior Champion 1973. Same season qualified for World final for the first time and scored maximum for England in World Team Cup final.
WORLD CHAMPIONSHIP RECORD: Finalist four times – 1973 Katowice 6 pts, 12th; 1974 Gothenburg 9 pts, 6th; 1975 Wembley 10 pts, 5th; 1976 Katowice 14 pts, 1st.
MAJOR HONOURS: World Champion 1976, European Champion 1974, Intercontinental Champion 1976, British League Riders' Champion 1974, 1975, British Junior Champion 1973, Wills Internationale winner 1974, Daily Mirror Grand Prix winner 1976, Northern Riders Champion 1974, 1975.
INTERNATIONAL HONOURS: Holds the record as the only man to have scored three consecutive maximums in World Team Cup finals . . . for England 1973, 1974, 1975. Has represented Young England, England, Great Britain, British Lions and Rest of the World.
LONG TRACK HONOURS: World 1000 metres Championship finalist 1974 and 1975. Winner of several individual meetings on the Continent.
GRASS-TRACK HONOURS: British 350 c.c. Champion 1971 and 1972. Winner of Strongbow British Grand Prix 1976.
CLUB HONOURS: Member of Belle Vue team that won British League Division One Championship 1971 and 1972, Knock-out Cup 1972, 1973, 1975, Inter-divisional Knock-out Cup 1975.

HOBBIES: No time for any!

FAVOURITE TV PROGRAMME: Top of the Pops.

FAVOURITE RECORDING STARS: Roxy Music.

FAVOURITE FOOD: Chinese.

FAVOURITE CAR: Mercedes.

FAVOURITE TRACK: Belle Vue.

FAVOURITE CLOTHES: Casual.

FAVOURITE COUNTRY VISITED: West Germany.

COUNTRY I WOULD MOST LIKE TO VISIT: South Africa.

IF I WASN'T A SPEEDWAY RIDER I WOULD LIKE TO BE: A promoter!

PERSON I MOST ADMIRE: The Prime Minister.

DISLIKES: Traffic jams, getting up in the morning and being beaten.

BIGGEST DISAPPOINTMENT: Not winning the World Championship at Wembley in 1975.

GREATEST THRILL: Winning the 1976 World final.

GREATEST INFLUENCE ON MY CAREER: Ivan Mauger.

HARDEST RACE: All of them.

BIGGEST REMAINING AMBITION: To stay World Champion and make a lot of money.

What it means to be World Champion by Peter Collins

Honestly, I still can't believe it! Months after my World Championship win in Poland, I am still finding it hard to accept that the dream has become reality. But it is a very nice feeling.

What does it mean to be Champion? Well, in the first place a mixture of elation and relief. Elation because I wanted to be World Champion so badly. Relief because I don't have to eat my heart out any more. Although many people say the pressure is on me now because I have to live up to being World Champion, I feel the pressure is off.

I am sure I will never again be a victim of the kind of tension I felt before the 1976 final in Katowice, something I go into in depth in another chapter. From now on I am going to enjoy my racing and, who knows, I may be even better for it!

That doesn't mean I am going to take my racing any less seriously or that I couldn't care less about hanging on to my title. I will be just as determined when the World Championship comes round again this season – but probably a good deal more relaxed.

I have only one attitude to racing and that is a desire to win. It doesn't matter whether it is a second-half scratch race or a World final. I still want to win. I will certainly be going flat out to keep my title in Gothenburg this September provided I qualify. After all, I have a long way to go to catch up with men like Ove Fundin, Ivan Mauger and Barry Briggs in the World Championship stakes.

What else does being Champion mean to me? In a word . . . money. I know money isn't everything but, next to winning the World Championship, it is No. 1 in my book. I make no apology for saying that I wanted to win the title as early in my career as possible so that I would get into the big-money bracket more quickly.

Why not? Only a few years ago I was an apprentice fitter. Before that, while I was still at school, I worked in a part-time job for two years to save enough money to buy a second-hand grass-track bike. I started at the bottom and, having worked hard to get to the top, I aim to make the most of it. After all, being a professional Speedway rider is a short-term career as in most sports.

I don't intend to finish at thirty-five with nothing to show for my years of racing round tracks all over the world. I want to make every penny I can.

Personally, I believe Speedway riders are underpaid. I would like to see the start and points money doubled for British League racing. But before the promoters jump down my throat and accuse me of being greedy, let me say I realize it would not be practical to pay that kind of money. I certainly don't want to see half the tracks go out of business.

But I believe the pay rates could be greatly improved in the World Championship. If I'd had to pay all my own expenses for last year's World final I would have finished well out of pocket . . .

Peter Collins with the World Championship trophy.

and I am the Champion! As it was, the only money worth talking about was the bonus start and points cash offered to the British riders by the BSPA.

We were on £20 a start and £20 a point, which considerably boosted the prize money. But I reckon the World final should be worth at least £5000 to the winner on the day.

These days, the really big money is on the Continent. Look at a fellow like Egon Muller of West Germany. He can demand a guarantee of £2000 for one Sunday afternoon meeting. When he rode for Hull Vikings in the British League last season he boasted that he could earn more in tips on the Continent than he was paid for League racing over here.

Having said all that, I admit I am one of the lucky ones. I have the backing of

West German super star Egon Muller . . . who can earn £2000 a meeting on the Continental long tracks.

many sponsors which means I have the very best equipment, engines, leathers, tyres, oil etc. At the other end of the scale you get the lads who only score a few points a meeting in the National League (Second Division) and who have to provide all their own gear. I don't know how they manage to make ends meet.

I am sure that sponsorship for the top British riders and the advent of the British-manufactured Weslake machine played a major part in ending England's long years in the World Championship wilderness. I certainly owe a big debt to Weslake. I was one of the first to use their four-valve engine and that gave me something of a start on the rest.

For years, English riders were at a disadvantage because men like Ivan Mauger, Barry Briggs and Ole Olsen had the backing of the Jawa factory.

There had to be other reasons, of course, why we had to wait fourteen years to win back the World Championship. Basically, I think we lacked the 'killer' instinct. Ivan Mauger was right when he said we weren't professional enough.

That has changed and, ironically, Ivan made life harder for himself by showing us the light. He, Ole and Barry set such high standards that a new breed of British riders, including myself, decided to copy them.

We realized we had to be more professional, more dedicated. We realized the importance of having the best equipment and maintaining it, of stripping down bikes before every meeting, of seeking out the assistance of top engine tuners and sponsors.

Even the young kids in the National League have a more professional approach today. Look how many have mortgaged themselves up to the hilt to get hold of four-valve engines. They want to compete at the same level.

The result is that we now have quite a few outstanding riders who are capable of winning the World Championship, riders who, on their day, are unbeatable. I am thankful that 5 September 1976 in Katowice was MY day!

Peter the Great

Richard Bott, Sunday Express *sports writer, broadcaster and business manager of Peter Collins, followed the Belle Vue and England star along the World Championship road last season and was in Katowice to share in his memorable triumph.*

You don't mind paying £12 for a bottle of Russian champagne when you have just become the manager of England's first World Speedway Champion for fourteen years! Even when there is nothing back on the empties!

I have been fortunate enough, thanks to my profession, to savour some wonderful moments in sport. But for obvious reasons none can compare with the feeling of pride and elation as Peter Collins completed his fifth and final race in Katowice's giant Slaski Stadium to win his first World crown.

I say first because there must be more to come for the brilliant young farmer's son from the Cheshire village of Lymm. Accuse me of bias if you like but find me a man who doesn't think Peter Collins was a worthy Champion on that September afternoon. And find me one who would dare to back against Collins ever winning the title again.

Some sportsmen strive a lifetime to reach the pinnacle of achievement. Most fail. Collins became World Champion at twenty-two, the youngest since 1955 when that other English hero, the late Peter Craven, won the first of his two titles. It does not matter whether Collins is as good or better than Craven, or comparable with Mauger, Briggs, Fundin etc. Champions should not be compared with one another. What matters is that they were good enough to win on the day . . . their day.

What was so memorable about Peter's triumph, what endeared him to the 100 000 crowd, English, Swedes, Poles, Russians alike, was the manner of his achievement. He rode the way he has always done . . . spectacularly, courageously, breathtakingly.

It riles me when people say, 'Speedway? Oh yes, I used to go but it was so boring and predictable. The first man out of the first corner ALWAYS won.' And they put heavy emphasis on the 'always'.

Well, all I can say is that if I had a fiver for every race I have seen Collins win from the back, I would be a wealthy man.

The very essence of his personality and appeal as a rider is his ability to win against the odds, to blend skill, courage and balance with an indomitable spirit, to do what looks impossible.

It is the same in any sport. Don't we feel far greater elation if our favourite football team come from a goal down to snatch victory in the last minute . . . if our horse comes from the back of the field to win in the last furlong . . . if our favourite boxer survives a knock-down and, when all seems lost, suddenly produces his Sunday punch to floor his unsuspecting opponent?

These are the thrill-makers, the chosen

Hail the new champ! Peter Collins is chaired by fellow English World finalists Doug Wyer and Chris Morton. Also in the picture are his mechanic George Clarke (left) and Belle Vue promoter Jack Fearnley.

few who have you on the edge of your seat, your heart in your mouth and leave you gasping in disbelief. Peter Collins is one of them.

No sportsman likes making hard work of winning. Yet Collins says: 'It gives me, personally, a far greater thrill to win from the back in the last twenty yards than to lead from start to finish. I know the fans like to see me win this way and I love to have a crowd behind me.'

There is no question that starting technique is very important in Speedway. Collins acknowledges that it is far easier to ride when you are out in front, because you can dictate the race, pick your own line . . . unless you make mistakes or don't take full advantage of the power at your disposal. The sharper your reflexes at the starting gate, the more points you should score . . . even if

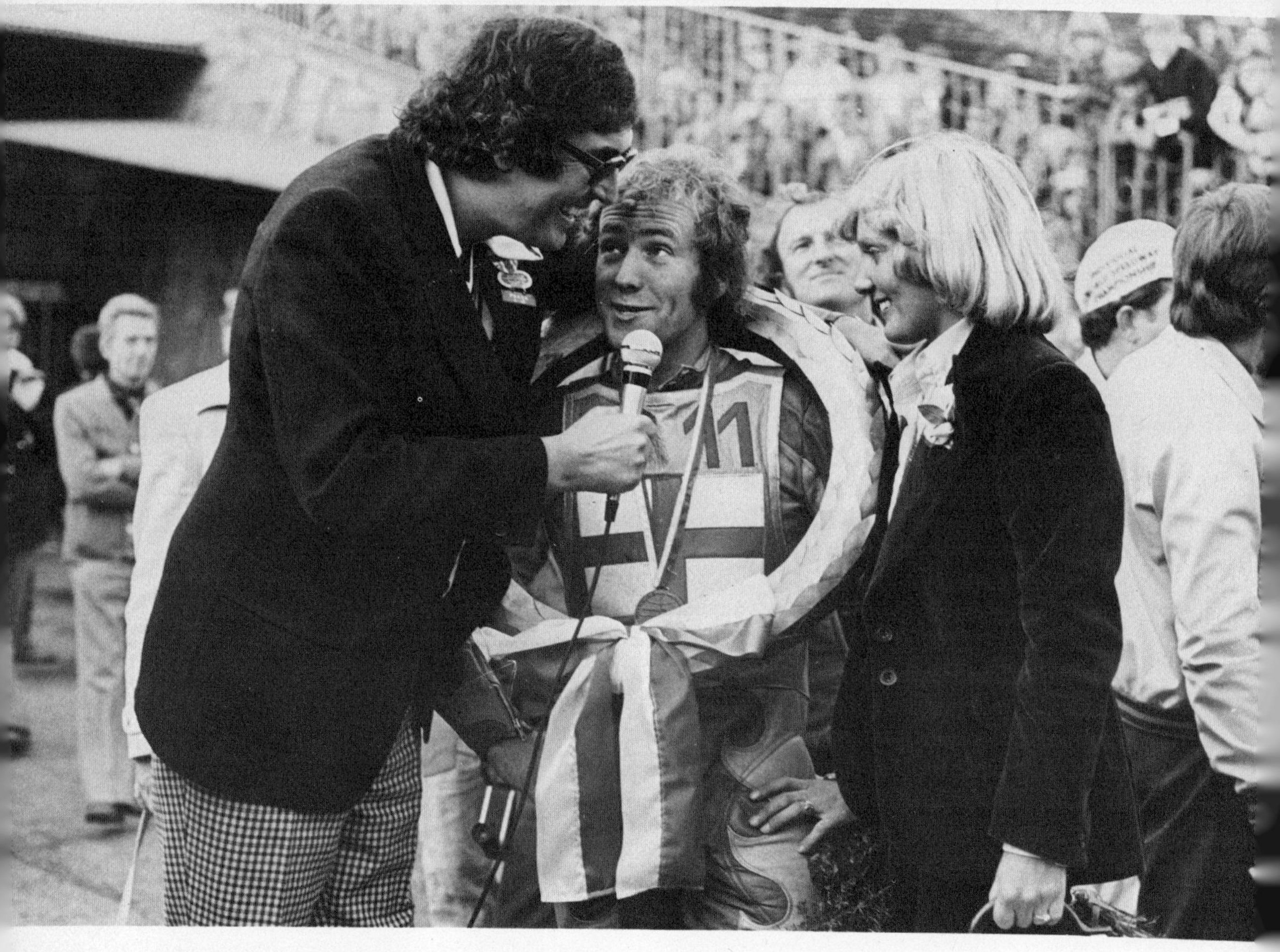

ITV commentator Dave Lanning interviews the new champion and his bride-to-be Angela Hilton.

you are not a very brave or accomplished rider. I have known a few riders who often win if they make the gate, but never pass anybody if they don't.

Collins has won hundreds of races from the gate, but he is not the fastest man in the world when it comes to dropping the clutch. 'Half the starts I make are good, the rest are rubbish,' he admits. 'But perhaps it is because I believe I have the ability to win from the back, that I don't concentrate sufficiently on my starting technique.'

The worry at the back of my mind – and it was shared by many others – was that Collins might never win a World title because of his inconsistent starting. What you can get away with in League racing and the occasional big event, you can hardly hope to get away with in a twenty-heat World final against the very best. Unless, of course, you ARE the best.

And in Katowice last September, Collins was.

But to get there he first had to surmount the hurdle of the British final at Coventry.

And that was a night that belonged to the fellow who must be labelled the unluckiest rider of the season, next to the ill-fated Swede Tommy Jansson.

You may ask how a rider who wins the Embassy Internationale the British Championship final and finishes runner-up in the world can be tagged 'unlucky'? But for Malcolm Simmons, the long, blond stylist from Poole, it was a season of so much achievement and so little acclaim. In the end, his outstanding contribution to the British Speedway year inevitably was overshadowed by Collins's victory in Katowice.

Simmons, who like Collins was backed by the Weslake factory, had previously been a 'nearly-man', always on the fringe of greatness. Suddenly, at thirty, he 'arrived'. He won his World Championship quarter-final, at King's Lynn, and the semi-final, at Leicester. He now had the confidence and the equipment to compete against the best and he outclassed the field in the British final with riding of the highest quality.

Collins finished fourth, edged out of the frame by his younger Belle Vue team-mate Chris Morton and that tenacious Yorkshireman Doug Wyer. But he did enough to qualify for the next stage of the competition, and, for him, that was enough. He produced a couple of breathtaking neck-or-nothing rides to snap up vital points and reinforced his reputation as the darling of the fans and the TV addicts.

He also reinforced the doubts in our minds that he was no longer England's great white hope for the World title.

Soon after the British final, I interviewed Collins for the *Sunday Express*. I put it to him that there was a growing school of opinion that he would never win a World final and that other English riders, like Simmons, Louis and Morton, were now as much of a threat to him as the Maugers and Olsens. 'Some people are saying you are "washed up" at twenty-two,' I told him.

Collins didn't know it at the time but it was an exaggeration of the facts, a deliberate and calculated attempt to kick his backside psychologically. As his friend and manager, rather than as a journalist, I wanted to shake him out of the belief that it would all come right on the big day.

It worked. And he admitted as much after the World final. But at the time of the interview he reacted angrily, as I hoped he would. 'Washed up?' he said. 'Is that what they think? Well, I'd better start winning a few trophies again. As far as I'm concerned, I'm still England's No. 1 and I'm going to win the World Championship.'

First, he won the Inter-continental Championship at Wembley on 26 June, on a broiling night in the midst of our heatwave summer. On paper it was a meeting of limited appeal, a 'nothing' title with eight to qualify for the World final. And after the Wembley disgrace the previous season, when the World final was staged on an apology of a track, it came as no real surprise that fewer than 30 000 turned up.

But those of us who did were treated to THE MEETING OF THE SEASON . . . an incredible night of shocks, sensations and superb racing. Race after race the form-book was turned inside out. And, thanks to the supervision of Hackney promoter Len Silver, we had a track worthy of the event and witnessed more passing and re-passing than at any Wembley meeting I can recall.

Here was the perfect answer to Speedway's critics, racing to stand your hair on end, the meat of a thousand arguments, shocks galore. It was, perhaps, the definitive Speedway meeting.

Not only did we see the statutory twenty heats but we also had the bonus of no fewer than three run-offs, one for first place, one for third and another for the vital eighth qualifying place for Poland.

Out of the World Championship on this night of drama went the title holder Ole Olsen and the 1974 Champion Anders Michanek, two of the biggest guns in the field. How could Olsen fail to finish in the first eight? How could Michanek, the only rider with maximum points after two rides, be eliminated? How could Collins, sensationally last in his first outing, win the meeting?

You had to be there in that Wembley hot-house to believe these things were happening.

Olsen, no stranger to World Championship gremlins, hit trouble from the start. He collided with Michanek at the start of heat four and was excluded 'for not keeping a straight course up to the thirty-yard mark'. Before we had time to digest that shock, Olsen was providing us with another. Out in the very next race, he bolted into the lead only for his engine to seize.

The great Dane, World Champion at Wembley the previous year, had three races left to salvage his hopes. But each time he had to give second best to an Englishman, Simmons, Collins and finally Louis heading him home.

Michanek, having virtually booked his World final place with two wins, threw it all away in his remaining races. His last chance came in the run-off for eighth place with Louis, the tiger from Ipswich. But a patriotic roar carried Louis home and as Michanek joined the also-rans we saluted the fact that we had five Englishmen in the World final line-up.

Collins, tailed off last in his first ride, was unbeaten after that and found himself facing the old master Ivan Mauger in a run-off for the largely insignificant title of Inter-continental Champion. But when he won it, it somehow put the cap on a glorious night for England.

It did more than that. It re-established Collins as our No. 1 hope for the World title.

AND SO TO KATOWICE and the Slaski Stadium, an arena as vast as Wembley but without the roof. We knew we had our best chance for years. No Olsen. No Michanek. In fact, no Scandinavians for the first time for twenty-five years. We had five finalists, Collins, Simmons, Louis, Morton and Wyer. And in the four-valve Weslake we had the engine to take on and beat the Czechoslovakian Jawa which had dominated for so long.

I don't want to dwell on the events too much because Collins himself, in another chapter, gives a graphic personal account of the races that mattered. His races.

Simmons was a very worthy runner-up but if there was a hard-luck story it was Mauger's. The brilliant New Zealander, so eager to equal Ove Fundin's record of five World titles, rode his heart out.

British Champion Malcolm Simmons.

SCB

Unlucky thirteen? Ole Olsen knows his World title is slipping away after a mechanical failure at Wembley.

But in his second ride, when he was lengths clear, his carburettor let him down. It was a sad sight to see him pull out of the race. But, on the other hand, it opened the door even wider for Collins and also gave Australia a chance of long-overdue glory.

Phil Crump took advantage of Mauger's misfortune to chalk up his second win and provided the greatest threat to Collins after the interval. Eventually, the young Aussie had to settle for third place over all but he was the first of his countrymen to stand on the rostrum

Peter Collins (nearest camera) and Ivan Mauger jet from the starting gate at Wembley in their run-off for the Inter-continental title.

since Aub Lawson was third in 1958.

So the day belonged to Collins and to England. Simmons finished only a point behind, Louis was sixth and our two World final debutants, Wyer and Morton, both acquitted themselves well.

Unbeknown to the 100 000 crowd, there was agitation and controversy behind the scenes when Polish officials claimed Collins was using an additive in his fuel. But an angry British pits crew pointed out that Collins was taking his fuel from the same tank as the other finalists and when samples were taken from the tank, the allegations were dropped.

If it was a deliberate ploy by the Poles to unsettle Collins, it failed abysmally. The Champion knew nothing about the fuel row until after the meeting. All he knew was that he had fulfilled the ambition of a lifetime.

He had won in the manner he loved, captivating his audience, demoralizing his opponents, with two breathtaking rides from the back of the field. I have a nice story to illustrate that reputation.

When the Polish charter plane, carrying Collins and a jubilant official British party, myself included, touched down at London's Heathrow Airport the following day, there was a call for the new Champion to alight first for the benefit of the waiting photographers.

As Collins pushed his way down the aisle to the front of the plane, ITV commentator Dave Lanning quipped: 'Typical Collins. Always has to come from the back!'

World final score chart 1976

							Pts
1	Peter Collins (*England*)	3	3	3	3	2	14
2	Malcolm Simmons (*England*)	2	2	3	3	3	13
3	Phil Crump (*Australia*)	3	3	2	1	3	12
4	Ivan Mauger (*New Zealand*)	3	e.f.	2	3	3	11
5	Zenon Plech (*Poland*)	1	2	3	2	3	11
6	John Louis (*England*)	2	1	1	3	2	9
7	Doug Wyer (*England*)	0	3	3	1	1	8
8	Egon Muller (*West Germany*)	3	1	2	2	f.	8
9	Scott Autrey (*USA*)	2	2	1	2	0	7
10	Jiri Stancl (*Czechoslovakia*)	2	2	0	1	1	6
11	Chris Morton (*England*)	1	1	1	2	1	6
12	Edward Jancarz (*Poland*)	1	1	0	1	2	5
13	Marek Cieslak (*Poland*)	0	3	0	e.f.	1	4
14	Jerzy Rembas (*Poland*)	1	0	2	0	0	3
15	Valeri Gordeev (*USSR*)	0	0	1	0	x.	1
16	Vladimir Gordeev (*USSR*)	0	0	0	0	0	0

Reserve: Anders Michanek (*Sweden*) 2 pts from 1 ride

f. – fell
e.f. – engine failure
x. – did not ride

Katowice–race by race

No one knows the drama of the 1976 World final better than the man who won it. Here, in his own words, **Peter Collins** *re-lives the five unforgettable races that took him to glory.*

Heat 3

Doug Wyer (*England – Red*), Peter Collins (*England – Blue*), Zenon Plech (*Poland – White*) and Jiri Stancl (*Czechoslovakia – Yellow/Black*).

I was off gate two and the first two heats had been won from gate one . . . where Doug Wyer was now sitting. I desperately wanted to get off to a good start but I was determined not to take any risks at the gate. I wasn't going to blow my chances with a tape-breaking exclusion.

But I was annoyed with myself for being pretty badly away. Stancl, who was only on a two-valve, shot out of the gate, with Wyer right up with him. I found myself in a very tight situation on the first corner and it amounted to just about my most anxious moment of the whole final. I could very easily have touched someone's back wheel and gone down. And that would have been the end of my World title hopes in the first few seconds!

I remembered being in a similar spot in the first race in the 1971 Second Division Riders' Championship final at Hackney. On that occasion I did catch a back wheel and down I went.

But this time I got round that first turn safely, though I was back in third place. I flew down the back straight and roared past Wyer on the pits turn. Then, as we started the second lap, I found the power to take Stancl. I needed to hit the front pretty quickly because I had taken a fair bit of dirt from the back wheels of Stancl and Wyer in that first lap, the track being a bit damp from the rain which fell during the opening ceremony. Once I was in the lead I had no problems and I managed to beat the new track record set by Egon Muller in the first race.

Perhaps I made hard work of that race but at least I now had the confidence that my engine was powerful enough to give me a chance if I missed the gate again.

Heat 7

Peter Collins (*England – Red*), Malcolm Simmons (*England – Blue*), John Louis (*England – White*) and Jerzy Rembas (*Poland – Yellow/Black*).

Undoubtedly my hardest race, not only of the final but of the season! And I had an idea it would be when I rode up to the starting line. Once again I was very anxious not to break the tapes yet I didn't want 'Simmo' or John to get away. The pressure was really on.

I had the inside gate but my two England team-mates beat me out of the trap. 'Simmo' was away like a rocket

Heat three . . . Collins (No. 11) is boxed in on the first corner and comes so near to disaster.

and he had done that to me twice in big meetings earlier in the season and I had been unable to make any impression on him.

This time I had to get past John as well. I had a tremendous first-lap battle with him and had to wait until the first corner on the second lap to dive under him. Then it was down to the business of trying to catch 'Simmo', who must have been thirty yards in front. But on the day my engine was terrific. Dave Nourish had tuned it to perfection.

I think it was just that bit faster than Mal's and I caught him at the end of lap three. Now it was neck or nothing. Going into the first corner on the last lap I just managed to force my front wheel ahead of Mal's and that was enough for me to have the advantage. It

Heat seven . . . Collins roars under British Champion Malcolm Simmons to score a classic victory.

was a tremendous feeling to take the lead.

I raced across the finishing line in a time of 72.2 seconds, another track record and one which was to stand for the rest of the meeting. Having come from the back twice and beaten two of my most dangerous rivals, I suddenly knew I had a great chance of winning the title. But I also realized that it was asking too much to win all my races from the back. You can only get away with missing the gate for so long and I knew I had to make at least two good starts in my three remaining races.

Heat 9

Edward Jancarz (*Poland – Red*), Chris Morton (*England – Blue*), Egon Muller (*West Germany – White*) and Peter Collins (*England – Yellow/Black*).

Once again I was cautious at the start but much more confident than I had been at the beginning of the meeting. Jancarz had only managed a couple of third places and Chris Morton, in his first World final, also had two points and faced his second ride in successive heats.

Muller had come to Katowice reputedly with the fastest bike in the world and had broken the track record in winning the first heat. It was his first World final, too, and how well he did to score eight points. But for a spectacular crash in his last outing he might have had double figures.

Considering the limited experience he had had on conventional Speedway tracks – he is a long-track specialist – he had a tremendous final and I have a lot of respect for him.

But in this particular race I managed to get my first decent start, from the No. 4 trap, headed Muller into the turn and controlled the race from then on. It was a very happy Peter Collins who went back to the pits still unbeaten after three rides.

One thing in my favour had been my draw number . . . eleven. It meant my rides were nicely spaced. I had also been able to watch the first two heats from the pits and to get an idea of the track – and the referee's methods!

Heat 14

Scott Autrey (*USA – Red*), Phil Crump (*Australia – Blue*), Valeri Gordeev (*USSR – White*) and Peter Collins (*England – Yellow/Black*).

I was on the outside again and I knew that Phil Crump was the one to watch. He had only dropped one point and had

Heat nine . . . Collins (left) broadsides round the first turn to hold off Egon Muller, Chris Morton and Edward Jancarz.

to beat me to have a chance of being Australia's first World Champion since Jack Young in 1952. But England had waited a long time too and I was in no mood to let the Championship slip through my fingers now.

I made a good gate – two on the trot; how about that? – and led all the way for my fourth win. The race was a bit of a disaster for 'Crumpie', who was edged into third place by Scott Autrey.

Now I had to sweat it out until heat 20, watching the races, checking the programme. I didn't have to worry about my bike because my team of helpers were doing such a great job.

Heat 20

Ivan Mauger (*New Zealand – Red*), Vladimir Gordeev (*Russia – Blue*), Peter Collins (*England – White*) and Marek Cieslak (*Poland – Yellow/Black*).

The big moment. I only needed second place to achieve my life's ambition. In fact, the way things had worked out for me I only needed third spot to have a run-off with Mal Simmons. But so much can go wrong. Would I break the tapes? Would I fall off? Would my engine suddenly let me down and rob me of my finest hour?

On paper I had the beating of Gordeev and Cieslak. And Mauger, the man I had feared and respected most, was out of the

Heat fourteen . . . another breathtaking first turn from Collins and it's the end of the World title hopes of Australia's Phil Crump (left).

RENOLD

Heat twenty . . . Ivan Mauger is out in front but Collins knows that World title is in his pocket.

running after an engine failure in his second ride.

I could feel the pressure building up inside me as I cruised to the starting line.

The tapes flew up and away we went. Ivan made the gate and all I wanted to do was get to the first corner ahead of the other two riders. Having done that I was happy. There was no way I was going to challenge Ivan in a bid to complete a maximum. I would have gladly settled for winning the title with ten points, if it had been enough.

That last heat seemed to go on for ever and all that kept flashing through my mind was, 'Will the bike hold out?' The last lap . . . the last corner. I was absolutely rigid on the bike, which is hardly following the coaching manual. But I was so terrified of falling off.

As I came into the finishing straight, still trailing well behind Ivan, I could see the chequered flag. I thought to myself, 'If the engine stops now I'll be able to coast over the line.' Then, as I got closer to the flag, I thought, 'Even if I fall off I can roll over the line.'

Then it didn't matter any more. I flashed across the line and I knew I'd done it. I WAS WORLD CHAMPION. The feeling was so fabulous, so unbelievable, I couldn't begin to put it into words. For a split second everything seemed to go black. Then I saw the marvellous English fans cheering their heads off and jumping up and down in their seats.

Ivan Mauger was waiting on the back straight to congratulate me. As I approached him I wondered what he was thinking. Did he consider me to be a worthy Champion? Did he think my win was a fluke?

Here was a man who had been such a great World Champion and who had set such standards for the rest of us to follow. I knew he desperately wanted to equal Ove Fundin's record of five Championships and how disappointed he must be to have lost his chance because of an engine failure.

Suddenly I felt that I was in new territory, Ivan's territory. Like him I had joined the small band of World Champions.

And whenever I think about being World Champion I will think of those five rides in Katowice. In terms of actual racing they added up to barely SIX MINUTES. But as long as I live I think I will be able to recall every single second.

My secret fear

Peter Collins *talks of the build-up to the 1976 World final, the fears and pressures, the people who made his triumph possible and the glorious aftermath of victory.*

The night before the 1976 World final in Katowice I felt as though I was inside a plastic bag fighting to get out. I have never known such tension. This was the final I HAD to win.

My secret fear was that if I failed – at the fourth attempt – I might never win the title. In fact, I was scared that I might never even qualify again!

Ever since I broke into big-time Speedway I had been hailed as a future World Champion . . . the golden boy of British Speedway . . . the great white hope. No one had really expected me to win at the first attempt, at Katowice in 1973.

But six points was a poor return and I hadn't done that much better in Gothenburg in '74. I went to that World final as European Champion but only scored nine points. Then, at Wembley in '75, many people had tipped me to win. I had a great record at Wembley and loved the place. I fancied my own chances very strongly. But after two fine wins, my dreams were shattered in a sea of mud after the track had been watered.

Defeat on that night, when the Wembley track was nothing short of a disgrace, knocked the stuffing out of me for a long time.

I had a good season in '76, leading up to the World final. But when I could only finish fourth in the British final at Coventry, people started to talk. They said my gating was always going to let me down, that other English riders, like Malcolm Simmons and John Louis, were now a better bet for the title.

That made me angry and even more determined to prove them wrong. I boosted my hopes by winning the Inter-continental final at Wembley on a night when the track was as different again from the shambles it had been the previous season.

But being Inter-continental Champion didn't count for much. It was nice but it was only a stepping-stone to the big one, the World title I had dreamed of winning since I was a kid.

Before I set off for Poland I was fairly confident. I had raced three times at the Slaski Stadium. The first time was in the 1973 World final, which I mentioned earlier. Then I had scored a maximum for England in the 1974 World Team Cup final and seventeen points in a Test match against the Poles in '75.

One worry, and a big one, was not knowing what I was going to ride. I was very busy riding in the weeks leading up to the final and that helped to keep the mental pressures off me. I simply didn't have time to think about Poland. But in the last couple of weeks I had to prepare myself and my equipment.

My last meeting in England, before setting off for Katowice, was a League match at White City and I planned to try out a new bike. It was a very wet

No worries now . . . Peter Collins gives the World Championship trophy a kiss during a night of celebration.

night and all sorts of things went wrong. My engine blew up. I only scored seven points. And I flew to Poland wondering which of my Weslake engines to use on the day. It was a big worry because unless you have complete confidence in your equipment you are at a distinct psychological disadvantage, particularly in a meeting as important as a World final.

But I regained my confidence in practice on the Saturday afternoon. The track was fabulous and my bikes performed perfectly. I enjoyed the practice so much so that I started using a bit of kidology. I deliberately made mistakes to try to make my opponents think the track didn't suit me. In my own mind I knew it was just what I wanted and when we packed away the bikes in readiness for the big day, I realized that I was never going to have a better chance.

There was nothing more to do but while away the hours between the practice and the meeting itself. That was when the mental pressure began to build up.

I have always had a reputation for being ice-cool under pressure. Ideal temperament. No nerves. But I can reveal that quite a few times over the years I have suffered from palpitations.

Suddenly, I feel a lump in my throat, my heart starts beating like mad and I find it difficult to breathe. It is not only uncomfortable but frightening. There have been times when I have felt so bad that I have had to go and lie down in the dressing-room between races.

It is particularly unnerving when it happens during a race. I have never felt like blacking out or anything like that but it has been bad enough to affect my concentration.

Doctors have assured me there is nothing wrong with my heart and that many professional sportsmen suffer from palpitations, as a result of the pressures. I could have taken pills but these would probably have had the effect of dulling my reactions and I couldn't afford that in a big meeting.

It is something I have had to learn to live with. I was worried about a recurrence in Poland but although the tension really built up inside me before the World final, my heart-beat remained steady.

I had enough to worry about as it was. That night, before the final, I seemed to be so near and yet so far from achieving my life's ambition. I knew I was one of the hot favourites, if not THE favourite.

In the crowded restaurant of the Hotel Katowice, people kept coming over to my table and shaking my hand, Germans, Poles, Swedes. 'Are you Peter Collins?' they asked. 'Good luck, P-e-e-e-t-e-r. You are going to win!'

But what if I failed? It was getting harder every year and, if I didn't succeed this time, it would get even harder. I began to make excuses in my mind. I thought how unfair it was that the World final was a 'sudden death' affair, a one-off meeting. Why didn't they run it on the lines of the motor-racing World Championship, I thought. Surely, it would be so much fairer to stage a big meeting in every principal Speedway nation with the Championship decided by a points table.

In fairness to myself, let me say I still feel that would be a more satisfactory method. But at the time it was an excuse, a scapegoat in the event of failure.

'Don't worry about it,' said my manager Dick Bott. 'You are only twenty-two. Think of Mauger, Olsen, Michanek . . . they were all older than you when they first won the Championship. Think of Louis and Simmons now. They are much older than you and must be more desperate to win.'

His words were no comfort to me. At that moment no one could have been more desperate, more impatient than me.

'Look, Dick,' I said. 'I don't want to wait until I'm thirty to be Champion. I want to win now . . . while I'm young enough to make the big money. I know I can beat all these riders; I have done it before. I MUST win tomorrow.'

I must have spent hours in the restaurant that night, doodling on dozens of serviettes, sipping a little wine to calm my nerves. Egon Muller came over for

Peter Collins listens intently to some words of wisdom from ex-British Champion Eric Boocock, who was a tower of strength in the pits at Katowice.

JAWA

Collins with Belle Vue team mates Russ Hodgson (left) and Alan Wilkinson.

a chat. He seemed to be very relaxed and I began to wonder what he and the others were thinking.

Dick Bott tried to pursuade me to go to bed but I didn't think I would be able to sleep. Eventually, he said: 'Have a look round. How many of the other riders can you see?' 'A few,' I replied.

'You can't see Ivan Mauger, can you? He's gone to bed. He's the real pro.'

That was good enough for me. Ivan was the rider I had always respected, always tried to copy. The complete, dedicated professional. I took the hint and went up to my room. Surprisingly, I slept quite well....

What a difference twenty-four hours can make. The next night I was back in that restaurant as the new World Champion. All the tension had gone, I was riding on cloud nine. People were singing and dancing, champagne corks were popping.

Collins and business manager Richard Bott, editor of the *Peter Collins Speedway Book*.

When Angie, my fianceé, and I came back from the official reception at the Slaski Stadium, there was an incredible party atmosphere at our hotel. And, amazingly, the Swedes seemed to be more excited about my victory than the English!

They were chanting my name so rhythmically that the band put it to music and suddenly everyone was on their feet dancing and clapping. I was in the middle. It was a fantastic experience.

The only way I can explain the enthusiasm of the Swedes is to say that none of their riders had qualified for the final – a very rare occurrence – and I had ridden with a lot of success in Sweden shortly before the final. I think they just decided to adopt me!

Yes, it was a wonderful night for me. But so many others deserved to share in my moment of glory. My Katowice triumph was the culmination of the efforts of a lot of people, my family, my sponsors, close friends like Colin Messer and Alan Cornes who own the garage in Lymm where I work on my bikes.

And what about the team I had with me in Katowice? There was Dave Nourish, who had done such a fantastic job tuning my Weslake engines beforehand and who spent the meeting checking the valves and points between races to make sure everything was spot on. There was my mechanic, George Clarke, who changed the tyres, fuel and oil. And there was my Belle Vue team manager Eric Boocock, who took the clutch to pieces after every race and who advised and encouraged me throughout, calling on all his experience as former British Champion.

If I had failed I would have failed them as well as myself. Perhaps they didn't have to share the burden of mental pressure but they certainly deserved to share my triumph. Without them I couldn't and wouldn't have won.

Wedding album

It was Speedway's Wedding of the Year and also the best-kept secret! World Champion Peter Collins and his bride Angela Hilton decided to dodge the limelight. No crowds, no TV cameras, no gimmicks.

They were so anxious to have a quiet wedding that they had the wrong church printed on the invitations. Guests were not informed of the switch from St Peter's RC Church, Middleton, Lancashire, to the chapel at De La Salle College, until forty-eight hours before the wedding – and then they were sworn to secrecy.

Sunday Express photographer Brian Scott was allowed to attend the reception to snap the happy couple cutting the cake but only official photographer George Hartley was at the service and he has supplied the other pictures for this exclusive album.

Reluctant bridegroom? Peter Collins gets some not so gentle persuasion from brothers Les, Neil and Philip.

Left: Arrival of the bride. Angela pauses on the steps of De La Salle Chapel with her father, Mr Wilfred Hilton, ladies in waiting Ann Collins (left) and Christine Brooks and bridesmaids Gillian Hilton and Sally Dervin.

Below: Peter slips the wedding ring on to Angela's finger.

Opposite: Father Sullivan shows the marriage certificate to the newly weds.

Left: Angela shows off her wedding ring to her ladies in waiting and bridesmaids.

Below: Wedding group. Left to right: Philip Collins, Mrs Mary Hilton, Peter and Angela, Mr Wilfred Hilton, Mrs Eileen Collins.

Opposite: Cutting the cake.

TENDER

How it all started

World Champion **Peter Collins** *looks back to his childhood days as a farmer's son, his first interest in motor cycles and his early days in Speedway.*

When I made my Speedway debut, at the age of 16, people were amazed by my 'instant' success. What they didn't know was that I had virtually lived on a motor bike for eight years!

I was lucky enough to be brought up on a farm with acres of open space. Dad was a motor-cycling enthusiast so it was natural that I should fancy having a go, particularly when my parents started taking me to Belle Vue Speedway every Saturday night.

After that, every spare moment was taken up broadsiding in the farmyard on a push-bike or roaring round the fields on a cut-down road machine. I was eight years old when I rode my first motor cycle, a 98 c.c. James. I must have ridden a dozen different bikes after that, before I started racing seriously on a track.

As far as I can remember, motor bikes were just about the only interest of me and my pals, lads like Dave and Chris Morton and Dave Trownson, who followed me into Speedway. I had other mates who raced with us round the fields but who lost interest when they got older.

You can't ride in competitive Speedway until you are sixteen, but depending where you live, there are usually junior grass-track competitions which give you the opportunity to learn how to race.

I took a part-time job when I was fourteen to save the money to buy my first grass-track bike. It was a Hagan BSA and cost me £100. That was a fortune to me in those days.

Halfway through my first season of racing on grass, I realized the 250 c.c. machine wasn't fast enough for the unlimited events. Eventually I drew out my life savings and gambled everything on a 500 c.c. Stacey Jap. It was worth it because I won quite a few events.

But when I started in Speedway in 1970, I didn't have the financial backing that some of today's kids are fortunate enough to have at the start of their careers. In fact, after a few impressive second-half outings at Crewe that year, I blew up my engine and when Crewe wanted to sign me I had to say, 'Sorry I can't.' I had no money and no bike.

By now I had left Broad Oak County Secondary School and was working as an apprentice fitter. But I wasn't earning enough to finance myself at Speedway. Then I was lucky enough to find my first sponsor, a local businessman called Jim Rowlinson. He had seen me in action and offered to sponsor me with grass-track engines for the following season. And I have a lot to thank him for, because I won the British 350 c.c. Grass-Track Championship in 1971 and again in '72.

Jim also offered to sell me a Speedway

bike quite cheap. I had to borrow the money from a friend and pay him back monthly out of my wages, but it was worth it because I desperately wanted to get into League racing.

I bought my first Speedway bike and rode it at the famous Belle Vue training school in the winter of 1970–71. The Aces signed me up and when the season started they loaned me out to their nursery team Rochdale Hornets. I must admit I took to Speedway as if I'd been doing it all my life. I suppose, in some respects, I had.

It certainly didn't seem any harder than it had looked from the terraces but then my grass-track experience and all those years of belting round the fields stood me in good stead. I had a very good first season and even got a few First Division outings with Belle Vue because they had one or two of their regular riders injured.

By now I realized I had a good chance of making the grade in the sport and packed in my job as a fitter before finishing my apprenticeship. If you are going to get to the top you have to have a professional outlook and that means riding full time.

People have said I was a 'natural'. No doubt I have a certain amount of natural ability. But, basically, I put my success down to starting very young and learning how to handle a racing bike by trial and error. I certainly had my share of bumps and bruises when I used to race round the fields.

I broke my leg in two places when I was fourteen. I was off school for more than six months. Then, a year to the day after my accident, I fell off again and broke my collar-bone. But those mishaps didn't deter me in any way. By then I was so determined to be a Speedway rider – and a World Champion – that I wasn't going to let a few broken bones frighten me.

Teams of the season

by Richard Bott

Pride of place must go to Australia . . . World Team Cup winners on their first-ever appearance in the final. They scored a famous victory in a competition which left England, the host nation, with egg all over her face.

We were the defending Champions, runaway winners in West Germany the previous year. For four years before that, under the banner of Great Britain, we had dominated the World Team Cup and been finalists every year since the inauguration of the competition in 1960.

With the 1976 final to be staged in England at London's plush White City Stadium, the sponsors were licking their lips for what looked a guaranteed money-spinner . . . until Australia threw a spanner in the works in the UK qualifying round at Ipswich.

16 May was, indeed, Black Sunday for England. The qualifying round we thought would be a cake-walk – after all, we had Peter Collins, John Louis, Malcolm Simmons and Dave Jessup – turned sour on us as the eager-beaver Aussies cashed in on our errors.

No wonder they were so determined. They had been thrashed out of sight on their own tracks in the 1975–6 Test series Down Under. Revenge could hardly have been sweeter. England literally crashed out of the competition, with Louis and Jessup both taking tumbles in crucial races. The Aussies, brilliantly spearheaded by Ipswich rider Billy Sanders, who recorded a maximum, finished with forty points, five more than England's sorry quartet.

Scotland, with twelve and New Zealand, with eight, brought up the rear but all the shame was England's. The organizers couldn't believe it . . . a World Team Cup final in England but with no England team!

Understandably, there was not exactly a stampede for tickets as the September final approached. Australia, Sweden, Poland and Russia simply weren't box office without England. In desperation, the organizers sought to turn the afternoon into a gala. They hired acrobats, gymnasts, brass bands, trampolinists, high divers and clowns in an attempt to whet the public's appetite. But their festive dish lacked the most vital ingredient.

Not that the sparsely-covered terraces worried the Australians as they chased their first ever World Team Cup success. They started favourites this time and though the plucky Poles pushed them hard, giving one of their best-ever team performances on a British track, the Aussies survived.

Phil Crump, third in the World individual final a fortnight earlier, made the difference, winning three of his four outings. He was only headed by Anders Michanek, who gave a superb solo performance for Sweden. With solid support for 'Mich', the Swedes could have won.

But frankly, there was only one real

World Team Cup winners Australia. Left to right: Phil Crump, Billy Sanders, John Boulger, Phil Herne, Garry Middleton and team manager Peter Moore.

loser in last year's World Team Cup . . . ENGLAND!

On the domestic scene two club sides lodged equal claims to be recognized as team of the season . . . *Ipswich Witches* and *Newcastle Diamonds*.

The Ipswich success story continues. Champions of the Gulf British League in 1975, one point ahead of Belle Vue, the Suffolk squad proved even more formidable last season. Unbeaten at home – in fact, they boasted a 100 per cent record again – they won nine of their away meetings to finish seven points clear at the end of the League programme.

Belle Vue again were reluctant runners-up and rubbing salt in their wounds was the fact that Ipswich also ended their

Ipswich . . . British League champions and Knock-out Cup winners. Left to right (standing): Ted Howgego, team manager Ron Bagley, Tony Davey, Trevor Jones and Dave Gooderham. (Front) Billy Sanders, John Louis (on machine), and Mike Lanham.

Knock-out Cup hopes at the semi-final stage. The Witches went on to beat King's Lynn in the two-legged final, to complete a wonderful double.

Peter Collins comments: 'In the first place, Ipswich had some good luck. They lost a five-points man (Mick Hines) from their 1975 side, whereas we lost a nine-points man (Soren Sjosten). So Rider Control gave us a rougher deal.

'Having said that, Ipswich by far and away proved themselves the best team in the League and Cup. They were more consistent and they had greater strength in depth. Our problem was that we had a long tail.

'I admire Ipswich for the way they have built up their team and have fought

Opposite: Peter Collins.

Warner
SPORTS
13

READING
3
READING
7

Opposite top: King Peter! Newly-crowned World Champion Peter Collins after his Katowice triumph, flanked by runner-up Malcolm Simmons (left) and Australia's Phil Crump, who was third.
Above: Peter Collins leads John Boulger during the World Team Cup qualifying round at Ipswich.
Opposite below: Action from Leicester versus Reading with England international John Davis out in front for the Racers. Chasing hard are (left to right) Greg Szczepanik, Boguslaw Proch and Ila Teromaa.

against using guest riders.'

That commendable policy might have back-fired if Ipswich had not been so fortunate in another respect. Apart from a worrying spell when skipper John Louis was nursing a dislocated collar-bone, they remained virtually injury-free. But they say you make your own luck and no one could deny Ipswich their success.

They found an adequate replacement for Hines in Dave Gooderham, who averaged 5.71 in League and Cup, and

Opposite: Speedway's Wedding of the Year! Peter Collins and his bride Angela Hilton.

Newcastle . . . New National League king-pins. Left to right: (standing) Tom Owen, Tim Swales, Mike Watkin, Joe Owen, Ron Henderson and Andy Cusworth. (Front) Robbie Blackadder, Brian Havelock (transferred to Workington during the season) and Phil Michelides.

they never lost by more than four points away from home. They also completed their title repeat in style by clinching the Championship at Belle Vue.

Skipper Louis topped the national averages and Billy Sanders and Tony

'Shrimp' Davey, backed him to the hilt. Behind them, second strings Mike Lanham, Ted Howgego and Gooderham did their stuff and Kevin Jolly and Trevor Jones also contributed to the Championship drive.

The Knock-out Cup competition provided Ipswich with a few frights before they overwhelmed King's Lynn in the final, winning both legs. Cradley stunned them, only losing 39–38 at Foxhall Heath in the first round. But Ipswich won convincingly at Cradley in the return.

Swindon proved even more redoubtable opponents in the next round and there were only two points in it on aggregate. Then came Belle Vue and two memorable semi-final matches. The first leg, at Ipswich, saw the Suffolk outfit claim

Former World Champion Barry Briggs (left) came out of retirement to spark a revival at Hull. West German star Egon Muller also made an impact during his brief stay at The Boulevard. But the man making his point here is Vikings favourite Mitch Graham.

an eight-point advantage. Belle Vue were sure they could pull that deficit back in Manchester but they didn't have the all-round strength and Ipswich went through to the final, 80–76 on aggregate.

The final was as good as over after Ipswich had won 41–36 at King's Lynn in the first leg but it didn't put a damper on the second-leg celebrations.

The freak result of the season was Ipswich's 40–38 defeat at Workington in the Inter-divisional Knock-out Cup. The humble New National League team succeeded where so many senior division sides had failed. In fact, *Workington Comets* have a legitimate case for being included among the teams of the season because these Cumbrian 'giant-killers' also sent King's Lynn crashing out of the Inter-divisional Cup. How about that . . . the two finalists in the British League KO Cup competition beaten by a 'Second Division' team in another major tourney!

But there can only be one choice from the New National League . . . *Newcastle Diamonds*. The Tyneside giants swept all before them as they gobbled up trophy after trophy . . . the League Championship, the Knock-out Cup, the Four-team Championship.

Frankly, they were too good. No one could live with the marauding Diamonds in the bread-and-butter League competition. They smashed one record after another in running up an incredible points tally of 61 out of a possible 68.

They won the Championship by no fewer than TWELVE points and finished TWENTY ahead of the third-placed team!

But their application for election to the British League in 1977 was rejected on a majority vote and they can be expected to terrorize the National League again. Well, perhaps not quite so much. This time they won't have Joe Owen!

This twenty-year-old farmer's son from Ormskirk, Lancashire, who had begun his career with Barrow, topped the New National League averages with an astronomical 11.55, held the Silver Helmet Match Race title FOR THE ENTIRE SEASON and crowned a glorious year by winning the Riders' Championship at Wimbledon. In fact, it would have been a sensation if he hadn't.

Now Joe steps up into the British League and Newcastle's loss is Hull's gain. He has already displayed his talents at senior level and is expected to emerge as one of the stars of the British League in '77.

But Newcastle, the team he leaves behind, were no one-man band last season. Almost as formidable as Joe was elder brother Tom, who took over the captaincy of the Diamonds during the season when Brian Havelock was transferred to Workington.

Tom Owen was runner-up in the national averages, with 10.28, but could not take part in the Riders' Championship because of the one-rider-one-club ruling.

The Diamonds, backed by go-ahead promoters Ian Thomas and Brian Larner, and shrewdly team-managed by former Halifax and England international Dave Younghusband, had second strings who would have commanded heat-leader slots in lesser teams.

Ron Henderson, promoted to heat-leader status when Havelock was transferred, missed eleven League matches because of injury but still averaged 8.69. Fellow Australian Phil Michelides (7.94) and Robbie Blackadder (6.64) also piled up the points, as did Yorkshireman Andy

Gulf
BELL
HELMETS

Cusworth (7.72). Even Tim Swales, seventh in the Diamonds averages, was a near-six-points man.

Yes, the Diamonds really sparkled in their second season as a New National League outfit. Ian Thomas's gamble in re-introducing the sport at a venue where the fans had been used to the very best – Mauger, Olsen, Michanek etc. – was totally vindicated.

Honourable mentions in the 'Team of the Season' category must go to *Coventry, Swindon, Hackney* and *Hull* in the British League and to *Ellesmere Port* and *Rye House* in the New National League. I have already handed Workington a well-deserved bouquet for their exploits in the Inter-divisional K O Cup.

Coventry take a bow for a major revival of fortunes in what was Nigel Boocock's farewell season. The primary reason for their leap from sixteenth place in 1975 to fourth in '76 was, however, the acquisition of reigning World Champion Ole Olsen.

Olsen, after a lengthy association with Wolverhampton, was originally allocated to Hull but insisted on a move to Coventry. The alternative, he threatened, was his non-participation in the British League.

Coventry eventually got their man and also the accomplished Czechoslovakian international Jiri Stancl. And with tiny Mitch Shirra emerging as a very real talent, the Bees were a match for anyone and enjoyed a highly successful season.

Swindon, 'wooden spoonists' in 1975, got off to an electrifying start and headed the table for a while. They eventually finished a very creditable fifth. Martin Ashby didn't have to do it all on his own for a change. Bob Kilby, Soren Karlsson, Bobby McNeil, Jan Andersson and Geoff Bouchard all rallied to the Robins's cause and the Wiltshire fans had something to shout about at last.

Hackney merit a mention for their revival, too. Seventeenth in 1975, they climbed ten places. They had a good, hard-working squad which included Polish star Zenon Plech. But it was the emergence of Dave Morton, elder brother of Belle Vue's Chris, as a world-class performer which was the biggest single factor in their success story.

A week or two before the 1976 season dawned *Hull* only had one rider on their books. They had lost out in the battle for Ole Olsen and looked destined to ride all season with a guest at No. 1. But promoters Thomas and Larner pulled off a major coup. They lured Barry Briggs out of retirement!

The result was staggering. Briggs found a new lease of life and also inspired a very new-looking Vikings squad in which Frank Auffret, American import Mike Curoso and ex-Halifax second string Graham Drury all made their mark.

Briefly, and at considerable expense, the Vikings found another crowd-pleaser in World long-track champion Egon Muller. No promoters could have made a greater effort to build a team and the Vikings were rewarded when they won their first-ever trophy, the Inter-divisional Cup.

Ellesmere Port were a very average outfit in the New National League in 1975 but they made rapid strides last season. They chased Newcastle as hard as they could and eventually took the runners-up spot, eight points ahead of third-place Workington.

John Jackson, who shared his favours

Swindon star Martin Ashby.

between Ellesmere and Wolverhampton, joined forces with young Chris Turner to win the New National League Best Pairs title from hot favourites Tom and Joe Owen of Newcastle.

The Gunners also pulled a master-stroke in signing sixteen-year-old Philip Collins, right under the noses of Belle Vue. Keep an eye on him in '77!

Finally, a pat on the back for *Rye House* who also enjoyed a revival of fortunes. Their star was Ted Hubbard, who took third place in the New National League Riders' Championship. But one star never made a constellation and, as with all the other teams I have mentioned, the secret of their success or near-success was strength in depth. That's how it should be.

Meet the family

Peter Collins *is the eldest of six children born to Cheshire farmer Bill Collins and his wife Eileen. Peter introduces the four brothers who could follow him to the top of the Speedway tree, the sister who has found success in another sport and the 'Super Mum' behind this incredibly talented family.*

Just think. In a few years' time there could be five Collins brothers riding in the British League!

Several pairs of brothers have been successful in Speedway. You can go back

The women in a World Champion's life . . . 'Super Mum' Eileen Collins and Peter's wife Angela.

pre-war to the Langtons, the Milnes, the Parkers. When I started my racing career, Eric and Nigel Boocock were England's leading duo. More recently, two lads I grew up with, Dave and Chris Morton, have come to the fore. Then there's Tom and Joe Owen.

The only trio of brothers I can think of in present-day racing are Gordon, David and Barney Kennett, from Kent. But I reckon if *my* four brothers eventually join me in the British League, we will be candidates for the *Guinness Book of Records*.

The only tragedy is that Dad, Bill Collins, didn't live long enough to see me win the World Championship or to see Les and Philip start to make the grade. Dad suffered a heart attack in 1975 and his death put a lot of extra pressure on Mum. No wonder the Press lads call her 'Super Mum'!

I'm out of the way now, since my wedding in November, but I haven't forgotten how hectic it can be in the Collins household in Lymm. For one thing the phone never stops ringing. Mum has to cope with the calls, keep the diary up to date, answer our fan mail, chauffeur the younger ones to grass-track meetings, repair our leathers and do a thousand and one other jobs on top of being a normal housewife. We all have a lot to thank her for.

Perhaps she gets her satisfaction out of seeing us do well on the track. I know she will be very proud if we all make it to the top.

Leslie has already got his foot on the ladder. He will be nineteen this year and has joined me in the Belle Vue team after two very good years in the New National League or what I call the Second Division.

He won a few prominent grass-track meetings before starting his Speedway career with Crewe in 1975. Last year, when Crewe closed, he moved to Stoke and did so well that he represented the Potters in the New National League Riders' Championship. He also turned in some very impressive performances for Belle Vue and earned the chance to get a regular place in the team this season. I certainly think Les has the potential to get right to the top. In fact, I'm going to have to be careful he doesn't steal my thunder this season!

Philip was itching to get into League racing last season and Ellesmere Port put him in their team as soon as he reached his sixteenth birthday. A former schoolboy grass-track Champion, he took to Speedway without any trouble at all and showed a lot of promise towards the end of the season. If he continues to progress at the same rate he could be making his bow in the British League this year.

Next in line is *Neil*. He will have to wait until the beginning of the 1978 season to be old enough to start League racing but there is no doubt he intends to follow in the footsteps of Les, Philip and myself.

Neil is already showing up very well in schoolboy grass-track events and has a nice style.

That leaves *Stephen*. Well, he's only ten so it's too early to say whether he will want to follow us into the sport. But, would you believe, he's already been riding motor bikes for four years!

We have one thing in common. We all started racing, or riding, very young. That is a tremendous advantage because some of the lads who come into the sport

Following in Peter's footsteps . . . three of the Collins brothers, Neil, Les and Phil.

shane

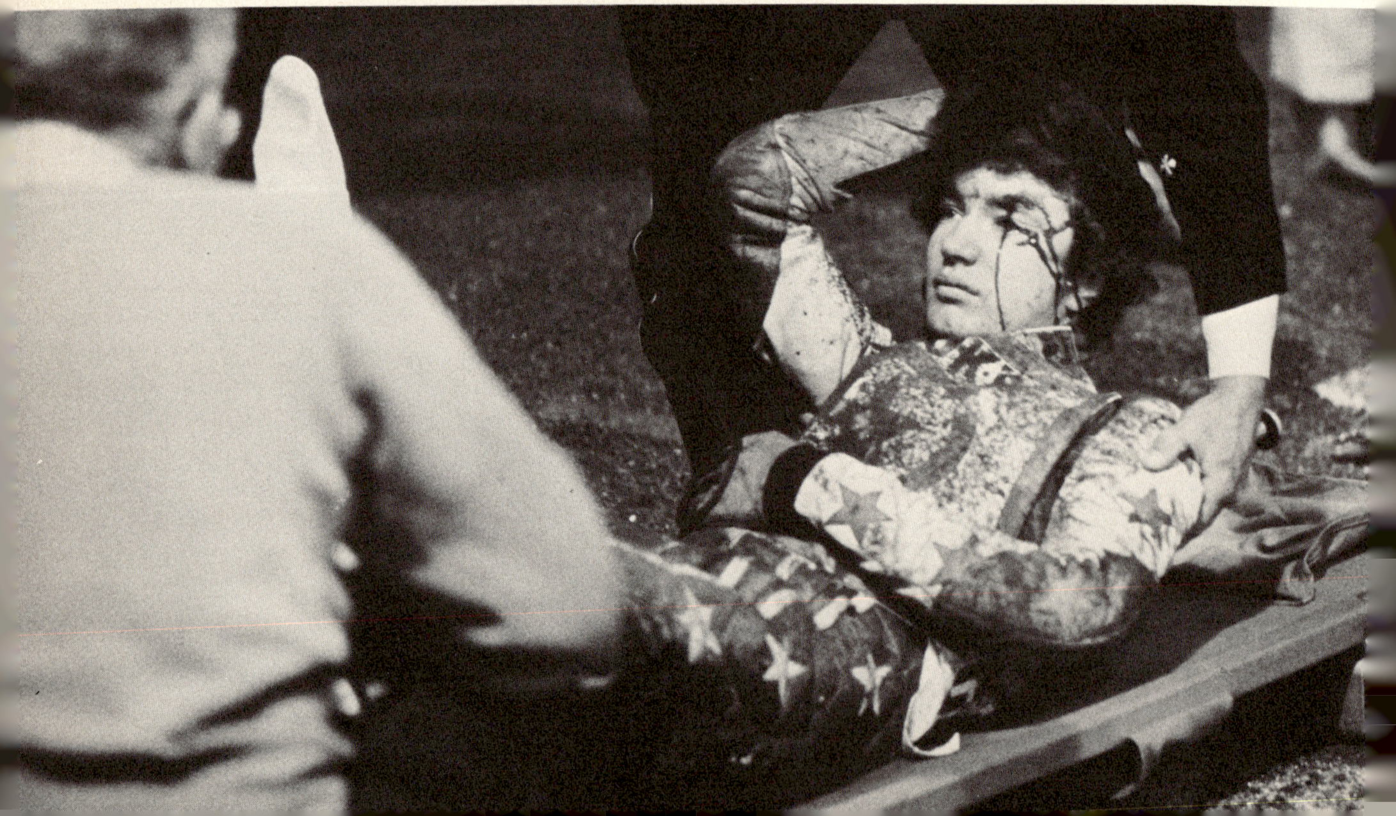

don't know what it's like to sit on a motor bike until they are sixteen or seventeen.

All my brothers seem keen to go into Speedway. There has been no pressure on them to follow in my footsteps. We just seem to be a motor-cycle-minded family.

It will be interesting to see if they develop their own riding styles. People say Les rides very much like I do and I suppose it is natural that he should have picked up some of my characteristics. But, to be honest, I have such a hectic racing schedule that I am rarely around to give my brothers advice. So what Les and Philip have achieved so far is down to them. They are virtually self-taught.

Phil Collins comes a cropper.

Opposite above: Dynamic duo . . . Les and Peter Collins in action for Belle Vue against White City.

Opposite below: Unhappy night for Les Collins . . . stretchered off with a gashed eye after being injured in the New National League Riders' Championship at Wimbledon.

It's a good job they don't allow women in League racing, otherwise my twenty-year-old sister Ann might show us all up! Seriously, though she has taken part in a novelty race for ladies, her sport is show-jumping. She prefers to ride horses rather than motor bikes and she has got quite a few trophies. I don't know whether she has any aspirations to get to the top in show-jumping but she is certainly improving.

Well, there you are, the Speedway family Collins. And perhaps in a few years' time I'll be wishing I didn't have so many brothers. One thing is for sure, there is no danger of my becoming complacent.

Ann Collins . . . ready for a spin at Belle Vue.

Speedway round the world

Peter Collins *talks about some of the countries he has visited in his racing career.*

Before I became a Speedway rider my only experience of travelling abroad was a school ski-ing holiday in Austria. I wanted to see some of the world and I am glad to say that I have had the opportunity through Speedway. Here are a few thoughts about the various countries I have visited – looking at them purely from the racing point of view.

Australia

I can't think of a better way to spend the winter than going out to Aussie. If you go out in the official British Lions party, you don't have to worry about getting bookings and although you only race

Ole Olsen (centre), the dashing Dane who did so much for Coventry last season, is seen here admiring the Midlands Cup with Coventry promoter Charles Ochiltree, team manager Mick Blackburn and Czechoslovakian star Jiri Stancl. Peter Collins rates Olsen's Vojns track in Denmark the best he has ever ridden.

3

Russia's Anatol Kuzmin consoles fellow-countryman Grigory Chlynovsky.

once a week, you can earn enough to live on and, if you're lucky, enough to bring some back at the end of the Aussie season.

If you stay at home in England, you tend to spend all the money you made the previous season and you just mess about half the time. Some riders say it is too much of a strain to ride all the year round. But most of the time I'm in Australia, I spend lazing on the beach, swimming or surfing. You get loads of free time out there.

I think Newcastle and Liverpool are my favourite Australian tracks, though it's quite an experience racing at Perth, which must be the biggest track in the world.

New Zealand

A lovely country and the racing is much the same as Aussie, the tracks being slightly bigger than in England. It has often intrigued me how a place the size of Christchurch has produced three World Champions, Barry Briggs, Ronnie Moore and Ivan Mauger.

I suppose it's just a coincidence. What I do feel is that the young Aussies and Kiwis who come over to England tend to be that much more determined than our boys because they have got to establish themselves or go hungry. They also have fewer distractions because they don't have families to go home to at night.

Sweden

The tracks in Sweden are all good shapes and are generally very well prepared. I have been over there a few times and I did some testimonial meetings for Olle Nygren just before last year's World final in Poland. The World final is in Sweden this year and that means going back to Gothenburg where I finished sixth in 1974.

Naturally, I expect to do much better this time and at least I will know what engine to use.

Denmark

Ole Olsen's new 300-metre track at Vojns is the best I have ever ridden. He has had it built exactly the way it should be for Speedway. The shape is excellent, there is plenty of room for overtaking and it is great fun to ride. I thoroughly enjoyed my two trips there last year, riding for England against the Rest of the World and, later, for the Vojns individual classic.

I must say that there are some other good tracks in Denmark, like the one at Fredericia.

West Germany

Big tracks. Big pay-days. West Germany is definitely the place to go for top English Speedway riders. I'm hoping my World Championship win will bring me a load of extra bookings.

Long-track racing is the thing in West Germany and the competition is pretty hot. But when the promoters offer you enormous guarantees to fly out for a Sunday afternoon's racing, you are not

Overleaf: Long-track racing is all the rage on the Continent and draws huge crowds. Left to right in this action shot taken at Plattling are: Barry Briggs, John Louis, Egon Muller, Ole Olsen and Jan Odegaard.

6
2

MOTORS
BELL
3
3
8

Two big names on the European circuits . . . Sweden's Anders Michanek and West Germany's Egon Muller.

likely to refuse. Anyway I love the country. Of all the places I have visited so far, West Germany is the tops!

Some of the tracks are a bit rough but the Germans know how to 'dress up' a meeting. I give them ten out of ten for presentation.

USSR

My first-ever trip abroad as a Speedway rider was to Russia. I went with Belle Vue to Leningrad. It was a great experience. From the racing point of view I can't tell you much about Russian tracks because I only saw the one at Leningrad. It was similar to the average English track but with a lot more dirt and, instead of red shale, the surface was black coal dust.

Poland

Obviously, Katowice's Slaski Stadium now numbers among my favourite tracks – though, to be fair, it did even before I won the World Championship. I had had two very good meetings there previously.

Like most Polish tracks it is hard to weigh up the first time you go. There is hardly any dirt, the surface is very slick and you have to set your bike up just right. When you've done that, Polish tracks are very easy to ride.

USA

This year I sampled the Californian tracks but, until recently, my only experience of Speedway in America was at the giant Houston Astrodome. What a fantastic place that is!

You would think it would be impossible to have Speedway indoors, on a REAL track. Not for the Americans. They brought the track in, lorry loads of shale. Then they rolled, tyre-packed and graded it and we had a very acceptable surface and a track about 250 yards long.

The people who came to watch weren't really Speedway fans because we were just part of a kind of motor-cycle show. There was a different form of motor-cycle racing every day.

But it was good fun and a terrific atmosphere. In case you're wondering, extractors in the vast roof take out the fumes and noise.

Well, that completes my little trip around the world but I think I ought to finish this chapter by paying tribute to the incredible Ivan Mauger, for winning the World 1000 metres (Long-track) Championship last year – for the third time!

Ivan completed his hat-trick – to go with his four World Speedway titles – at Marianske Lazne in Czechoslovakia on 12 September. He pipped Ole Olsen by one point with the defending Champion, Egon Muller, third.

I was reserve for that final and was disappointed not to qualify, because I have been in two long-track finals. I didn't make the trip because it was only a week after my World Championship win in Poland. I was not mentally prepared and my long-track bikes were in pieces. I had concentrated all my efforts on the Speedway final.

Perhaps my attitude would have been different if I had not been reserve. But I will certainly be trying very hard to qualify for the long-track final this year.

Just for the record, here is the score chart from the 1976 final: I. Mauger (New Zealand) 26, O. Olsen (Denmark) 25, E. Muller (West Germany) 21, A. Weisbock (West Germany) 21, J. Stancl (Czechoslovakia) 16, Z. Kudrna (Czechoslovakia) 14, A. Michanek (Sweden) 12, C. Betzl (West Germany) 10, J. Angermuller (West Germany) 9, B. Briggs (New Zealand) 7, D. Godden (England) 5, H. Wasserman (West Germany) 4, W. Duden (West Germany) 4, E. Stangeland (Norway) 3, C. Samuelsson (Sweden) 1, S. Kubicek (Czechoslovakia) 1. Res: E. Sova (Czechoslovakia) 5.

Candid camera

Opposite above: Talking of cameras, what's that perched on Gordon Kennett's shoulder? The White City star is doing a spot of filming himself.

Below: One of these days I'll have an early night, says World Champion Peter Collins.

Opposite below: Sign here, please! Injured Halifax star Henny Kroeze collects Chris Pusey's autograph on his plaster cast.

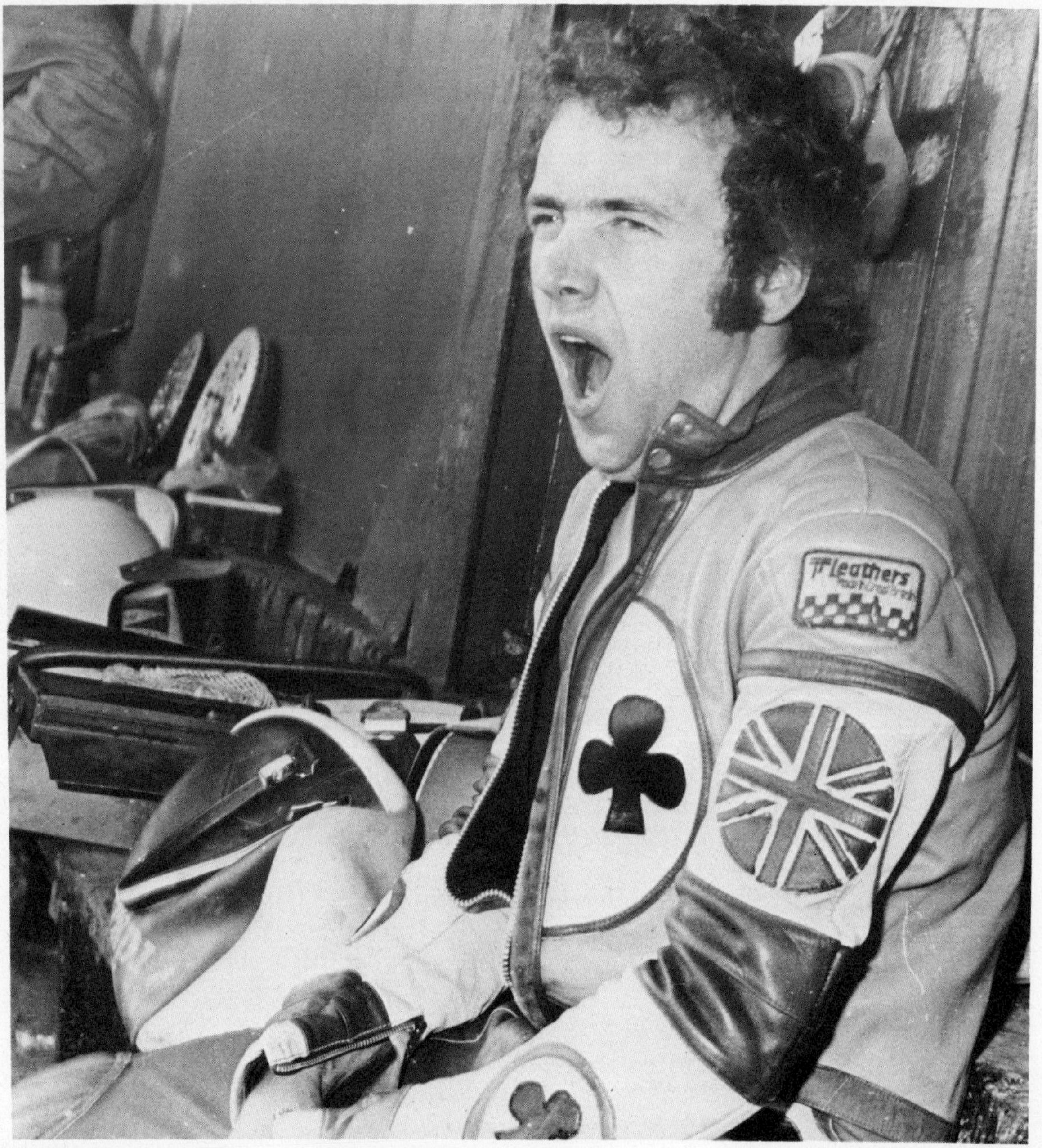

HAGON
BOSCH

Left and right: A double cover-up job . . . our first picture shows West Germany's Egon Muller keeping the rain off during the World final opening ceremony in Poland. And in picture two, Ipswich ace John Louis tries to cool off at Wembley on the hottest night of the year!

Below: Why are we waiting? Ellesmere Port's Chris Turner and Oxford's Carl Askew wonder what has happened to their team mates.

Peter Craven – England's last super star

by Richard Bott

They called him the 'Mighty Atom'. And he lived and died for Speedway. Peter Craven, England's last 'super star', World Champion in 1955 and 1962, fatally injured in a track crash at Edinburgh a year later, at the age of 29.

The first time I saw him off the track was at a presentation of awards at a London hotel in 1960. It was my first season reporting Speedway and I had seen little enough of the fellow on the track. But to see him standing there, barely five feet tall and baby-faced, like a schoolboy among men, I wondered how he could be such a potent force, such a feared opponent, in a sport demanding iron nerve, strength and skill.

And this was five years after he had won his first World title, at Wembley in 1955!

But Craven, like all truly gifted performers was a 'natural'. Where other bigger, stronger men struggled to control their bucking, roaring 500 c.c. Speedway machines, the tiny Craven made it look so easy with his immaculate balance and precise throttle control. He often hung from his bike like a Cossack horseman and there was no more spectacular sight in Speedway.

Peter Theodore Craven was born in Liverpool on 21 June 1934, one of boy twins. His brother Paul died at the age of three.

But Peter had another brother, Brian, two years his senior, and it was he who carried the family banner into the sport, when Liverpool's Stanley Park track re-opened in 1949.

Peter went along to have his first ride the day after his sixteenth birthday. He borrowed Brian's bike and promptly hit the fence, sustaining concussion. But the following season, 1951, Peter made eight appearances for Liverpool Chads in the old National League Second Division. He was no overnight sensation by any means and it was not until 1954, during his National Service, that he emerged as a genuine prospect.

Suddenly, he blossomed and not only topped the points chart for Belle Vue Aces, who he had joined officially in 1953, but qualified for his first World final. That year at Wembley, Craven scored three points, one more than the lowest scorer, Ove Fundin, who was also making his World final debut.

The following year, 1955, Craven was back in civvy street and on the brink of stardom. He had a brilliant season for Belle Vue and won through to the World final again. But he was a rank outsider for the title and when he won it, with thirteen points, he exclaimed: 'No one is more surprised than me.' He was England's first Champion since Tommy Price in 1949.

Craven was fourth in the 1956 final, dropping two points when his engine blew up and he had to push home for a third place. He was third in 1957 and could have been again the following season, but fell in a run-off with Aug Lawson and

The all-action style of Belle Vue's 'mighty atom' . . . the late, great Peter Craven.

Ken McKinlay. He made no impression in 1959, managing only seven points.

But by now he had become an international star, captain of England and a crowd-puller on both sides of the world.

I saw my first World final in 1960. It was Craven's seventh in succession – and he should have won it. We were all ready to cheer an English victory when Craven won his first four rides. But in a rough, tough eighteenth heat he was beaten by the tall, determined Swede, Ove Fundin.

Wembley was in uproar. Three men, Craven, Fundin and New Zealand's Ronnie Moore, the defending Champion, were level on fourteen points. Craven had the inside draw in the run-off but he had taken a knock in his final race and was still suffering from the ill effects. It showed when he trailed home third behind Fundin and Moore.

Oh, the frustration of dropping only ONE point in a World final, yet finishing third!

I didn't go to Malmo, Sweden, in 1961,

the first World final held outside England. Perhaps it was as well because it was a cheerless day for English Speedway. Fundin won again, Swedes occupied the first three places and Craven only managed six points.

But Wembley 1962 made up for all the disappointments. This time fourteen points proved enough. We had our doubts when Craven was beaten into second place by Barry Briggs in heat six, though Fundin was relegated to last spot in the same race. But Briggs had been third in his opening ride so it was up to Craven not to make any more mistakes. He didn't.

And as Manchester's 'Mighty Atom' climbed onto the rostrum to receive his £500 *Sunday Pictorial* cheque, 62 000 people roared their salute. We never dreamed we would have to wait fourteen years to see another Englishman crowned World Champion!

Perhaps you were at Wembley that night in 1962. Either way, you may be interested in the score chart from that last great occasion for English Speedway.

This is how they scored: PETER CRAVEN (*England*) 14, Barry Briggs (*New Zealand*) 13, Ove Fundin (*Sweden*) 10, Bjorn Knutsson (*Sweden*) 10, Ronnie Moore (*New Zealand*) 9, Ken McKinlay (*Scotland*) 9, Bob Andrews (*England*) 9, Gote Nordin (*Sweden*) 9, Soren Sjosten (*Sweden*) 8, Igor Plechanov (*Russia*) 7, Rune Sormander (*Sweden*) 7, Ron How (*England*) 6, Arne Carlsson (*Sweden*) 3, Mike Broadbanks (*England*) 2, Ron Mountford (*England*) 2, Pawel Waloszek (*Poland*) 2.

No one knew what fate had in store for Peter Craven a year later. He began the 1963 season in fine style, beating Golden Helmet holder Fundin when he challenged for the Match Race title. He rode for Great Britain in the World Team Cup in Austria and was top British qualifier for the World individual final. But it was an unhappy Wembley for him that year. He fell twice in his efforts to retain the title and saw the Championship go to Fundin again.

A week after losing his World title, Craven lost his life.

Riding for Belle Vue in a challenge match at Edinburgh's Meadowbank circuit, on Friday 20 September 1963, Craven lined up for the twelfth heat with team-mate Billy Powell against Edinburgh's George Hunter and Willie Templeton. During the race, Hunter's machine locked up and, in an effort to avoid the fallen rider, Craven clipped the stricken bike and crashed heavily.

He suffered very severe head injuries and lay in a coma in Edinburgh Royal Infirmary until he died at 9.10 p.m. the following Tuesday.

The Speedway world was numbed by Craven's death. The grief of his widow Brenda, their children Robert and Julie, family and friends, was shared by thousands.

The 'Mighty Atom' had gone and Speedway had lost more than a Champion. Peter Craven was 'Mr Nice Guy', cheerful, charming, unassuming, popular and respected by fans and rivals alike. His death created a vacuum in British Speedway which took fourteen years to fill.

And in the years to come, when, hopefully, we see other Englishmen crowned World Champion, we will not forget the little man whose illustrious career was so savagely cut short in its prime.

The day I lost my nerve

World Champion **Peter Collins** *makes an astonishing admission, revealing the real reason for his non-appearance for a British League match at Newport last season.*

Fear is something every Speedway rider has to live with throughout his career. But the dangers have to be accepted as an occupational hazard.

Normally, I don't worry about the possibility of being seriously hurt – or worse. I don't take unnecessary risks and I trust my equipment.

But I have to admit that one day last season, and for the first time in my life, *I lost my nerve!*

I was due to ride for Belle Vue in a Gulf British League match at Newport, on Friday 21 May. I didn't turn up for the meeting and it was widely reported at the time that my car had broken down en route.

My excuse was accepted and there were no comebacks – except that Belle Vue lost the match, 45–33. Well, my car didn't break down. I never left home. I ducked the meeting for one very good reason . . . I WAS SCARED.

I have never liked the Newport track. And I'm not alone in that respect. A lot of riders have been injured at Somerton Park.

But what finally made up my mind not to go had nothing to do with Newport. It was the news the previous night of the tragic and untimely death of Swedish rider Tommy Jansson.

I just couldn't believe it when I heard that Tommy, a great friend and rival, had been killed in a World Championship meeting in Stockholm.

It often takes a fatal track crash to bring home the dangers of Speedway to the riders as well as the public. But this one was too close to home in more ways than one.

Tommy and I were great pals. We had had a fabulous time in Australia the previous winter, swimming and water ski-ing. He was only a few months older than me and was a terrific rider – a future World Champion. Not only that but he was so safe on the track, never did anything silly. You can understand a rider being badly injured, even killed, if he is a bit of a lunatic. And there are a few Kamikaze pilots around in the sport.

But not Tommy. And when I heard he had been killed it really shook me up. The next day, when I was supposed to go to Newport, I was still badly shocked. I thought about how much I hated the Newport track and I made up my mind. There was no way I was going to ride.

Would I have gone if Tommy Jansson hadn't been killed? I don't know. I will never be able to answer that.

I raced at Newport later in the season, in the Knock-out Cup and again in the Golden Helmet. But they were more important than the League match. Belle Vue never do well at Newport in the League and I knew that a defeat there wouldn't be the end of our Championship hopes. But the Cup was different

Pete Smith (left) and Bob Coles in action at Newport . . . a track Peter Collins believes is dangerous to ride.

and, of course, the Golden Helmet is a big individual event.

What is it about the Somerton Park track that gives me, and so many other riders, the creeps? I'll tell you. In my opinion . . . it's DANGEROUS. The shape is all wrong. It has square corners . . . probably because it is constructed round the football pitch. But other tracks have been laid round football pitches and are safe to ride.

Sweden's Tommy Jansson. His death shocked Peter Collins out of riding in a British League match.

Imagine trying to control a runaway horse. Well, that's what it's like riding at Newport. You can't sit back and let the bike go, you've got to hang on to the handlebars like mad to keep control. If you don't, you are going to whack the fence.

I know, I've done it. If someone comes off in front of you there is hardly any room to ride round him without touching the fence.

When I went back to Newport last season to race against Phil Crump for the Golden Helmet, I had virtually convinced myself that the track wasn't all that bad. I was prepared to have a go. And as you know, I am used to coming from the back.

Crump made the gate on me so I tried to go inside him on the first corner. But, because of the shape, I found myself heading for the fence and I honestly thought I was going over the top.

I'm sorry I let my Belle Vue teammates down by not turning up for the League match. As it happened, they put up a hell of a show without me. But I know that any one of them might have opted out as I did, because we were all joking about it the previous week.

You can take it from me the Belle Vue lads were delighted to hear, during the close season, that Newport would not be operating in the British League in 1977.

As I said earlier, I'm not the only top rider with very strong views about the Somerton Park circuit. British Champion Malcolm Simmons forfeited a great chance of winning the *Daily Mirror* Grand Prix last season by refusing to ride a qualifying round at Newport. Until then he was unbeaten in the tournament!

But that League match is the only meeting I have ever missed through fear.

Generally, the dangers don't bother me because so many riders get up and walk away from spectacular crashes. Okay, cuts, bruises, broken bones are fairly commonplace but really serious injuries few and far between. And fatal accidents even fewer, thank goodness.

Why? Because unless you are a head case you don't take stupid chances. There are a few riders I could name who I like to steer clear of, either well in front or well behind. But most riders use their heads. When you all dive into the first corner it can be pretty hairy. But the man who has his wheel even fractionally in front has the advantage and the others simply have to back off. If they don't they are going to be the ones in trouble.

It's different if there is a gap to go through. I'm talking about riders going into a corner neck and neck. The one who can squeeze his machine fractionally ahead should be able to dictate the race at that point.

Obviously people take more risks in big meetings, particularly a World final. That's because winning is so important. But even then something has to give. It's all about getting your wheel in front. Then, if you're good enough and your bike is fast enough, you should be the boss.

I suppose there are times when a rider feels a sense of fear. But he would never show it during a meeting because it would give his rivals such a psychological advantage.

But I've got to own up to the fact that my bad moment came that Friday morning last May when a combination of shock at the death of a close friend and dislike of a track proved too much. At least it proved I'm human.

My six all–time greats

Peter Collins *looks into Speedway's Hall of Fame and writes about the six 'super stars' he rates as the greatest to race in his lifetime.*

Peter Craven

(*England – World Champion 1955 and 1962*)
I am proud to have the same initials as the late, great Peter Craven, to have ridden for the same club and to have emulated him in winning the World Championship. It is true to say that Peter was the rider who was my idol and inspiration. But for him I might never have become a Speedway rider.

From the moment my parents took me along to watch the famous Belle Vue Aces, when I was eight years old, I became one of Peter Craven's greatest fans. He sparked something off inside me because he was so spectacular, so thrilling

Five World Champions . . . left to right, Peter Collins (1976), Ivan Mauger (1968, 1969, 1970, 1972), Ole Olsen (1971, 1975), Barry Briggs (1957, 1958, 1964, 1966) and Freddie Williams (1950).

to watch. He was a 'natural', relying so much on balance.

We used to get to the track early and I would peep into the pits to see Peter preparing his machines. I remember the thrill when I got his autograph. Sometimes, during the meeting, I would walk round the track and watch him from different angles.

I was too young to go to the 1962 World final when Peter won the World Championship for the second time. But when he came back to Belle Vue with the winged wheel I was there cheering my head off. I never dreamed that one day I would be bringing that famous trophy back to the Manchester track. On second thoughts, perhaps I did!

What a tragedy it was when Peter was killed in 1963. But his death didn't deter me. I had seen enough to want to make Speedway my life and the man who fired me with that ambition was Peter Craven.

Barry Briggs

(*New Zealand – World Champion 1957, 1958, 1964 and 1966*)

The legendary 'Briggo' . . . eighteen World final appearances and Champion four times. What an achievement? If I do half as well, I'll be over the moon. How can anyone hope to match his record over the last twenty-five years? So many riders can turn in brilliant performances but, for consistency, 'Briggo' must be the tops.

I first rode against him in 1972 at Swindon. That was in the early days of my own career and I had a list of riders I wanted to beat. One of them was 'Briggo'. That night I beat him on his own track and I felt like a king. Perhaps he was having an off-night, but it was still a moment for me to cherish.

In recent years I have raced against 'Briggo' several times. Now I am sure he only rides for enjoyment and doesn't take as many risks or spend as much time on his equipment. But you still have to respect his skill and class. Even now you can see how he has superb control.

Ove Fundin

(*Sweden – World Champion 1956, 1960, 1961, 1963* and *1967*)

Another legend. And so far no one has matched his record of five World titles – unless you include long-track racing. I didn't see much of him when he was in his prime except in 1967, the year he won his fifth title. He rode for Belle Vue that year so I was able to admire his strength and style.

He is a hell of a nice bloke, too. I met him before the 1974 World final in Gothenburg and again in Poland last year. He gave me some good advice. I wish I had seen him ride more often but I saw enough to include him in my list of all-time greats. How could I leave him out with his record?

Ivan Mauger

(*New Zealand – World Champion 1968, 1969, 1970 and 1972*)

Next to Peter Craven, Ivan is the man I have admired most. He has done more for Speedway than anyone else, on and off the track. He started with nothing and

Great Dane Ole Olsen . . . . 'you can never be sure of beating him,' says Peter Collins.

COVENTRY
BEES
agv
BATES
COVENTRY
BEES

worked his way to the top, setting unbelievably high standards. His dedication and professionalism became an example for a whole new breed of riders to follow. Those who didn't were left behind. I have certainly tried to model myself on him, making sure my equipment is in perfect order right down to the last detail, trying to get myself into the right frame of mind for big meetings.

Ivan changed the whole image of the Speedway rider. He rid the sport of its 'Hell's Angels' reputation, dressed immaculately for sporting functions and spoke so articulately and forcibly as to win over the cynics who thought we were all grease and overalls.

On the track he became the super showman, with vividly-coloured leathers and stardust mudguards. But it always took second place to performance. And he is still one of the greatest riders in the world – and one of the fastest 'gaters'. That's Ivan, always setting the pace!

Ole Olsen

(*Denmark – World Champion 1971 and 1975*)

Like Ivan Mauger, a brilliant exponent of Speedway whether on conventional or long tracks. And another 100 per cent professional. I have always had the greatest respect for Ole because he has always known what he was doing. He has so much ability and is such a crafty rider that you can never be sure of beating him until you reach the finishing line. Give him half a chance and he will take it.

Ole is out on his own among Danish riders. When he won the World Championship in Sweden in 1971 he became Denmark's first World Champion at any motor sport, a national hero. Perhaps the knowledge that he carries so many hopes in his native Denmark has driven him on to stay at the top. I would say, of the current crop of world-class riders, he is definitely the hardest to beat.

Anders Michanek

(*Sweden – World Champion 1974*)

I am sure Anders would have been World Champion more than once if he had had the same determination as the others in my list of all-time greats. There can be no questioning his ability, though I think he has always relied more on brawn than some of us. He seems to drag the bike round but always looks as safe as houses.

His attitude towards Speedway has always been more of riding well when the mood takes him. He has enjoyed other interests and never allowed Speedway to take over his life. Anders once said: 'I enjoy Speedway but it is a silly game. Too many riders think of nothing else. All they think about is winning. That is stupid. You have to enjoy other things.'

But I am sure Anders has never been happier than when he won the World Championship in front of a Swedish crowd in 1974.

I have had some great races with him. In fact, one stands out as the greatest race of my life. It took place at Belle Vue in October 1973, after a breathtaking Knock-out Cup final second leg between Belle Vue and Reading. The teams had finished level on aggregate and it was decided that Anders and I should settle the issue with a match-race.

We were both handicapped. I had my left hand in plaster and had moved the clutch lever so I could operate both clutch and throttle with my right hand. Anders was on a borrowed machine

Ivan Mauger . . . the brilliant New Zealander who set examples for everyone else to follow.

which was not as powerful as his own.

The scales were ideally balanced and what a race ensued. Would you believe we passed each other on every corner on every lap before I just snatched the verdict by a few inches!

So there you are . . . my six all-time greats. Just imagine them all in one meeting and all in their prime. That would be something, wouldn't it?

Triumph for England's John Louis and Malcolm Simmons in the World Best Pairs. They are flanked by Denmark's Ole Olsen and Finn Thomsen (left) and Sweden's Bengt Jansson and Bernt Persson.

A couple of swells

Richard Bott *pays tribute to the 1976 World Pairs Champions John Louis and Malcolm Simmons, of England.*

Peter Collins didn't grab all the World Championship glory last year. England had John Louis and Malcolm Simmons to thank for a glorious triumph in the World Best Pairs Championship final at Eskilstuna in Sweden on 17 June. Our victory ended three years of Pairs dominance by the Swedes, who were particularly aggrieved to see that run come to an end on home soil.

But for the Swedes, the 1976 Pairs final was a meeting tinged with sadness. Eskilstuna was the home town of Tommy Jansson, the brilliant young Swedish international who had been killed in a track crash only a month earlier. Jansson had partnered Anders Michanek to success in the 1975 Pairs final in Poland and had also been part of a winning Swedish duo in 1973.

This time there was no Jansson and, because of a dispute over expenses, no Michanek. So the Swedes had to fall back on two other experienced internationals, Bengt Jansson (no relation) and Bernt Persson. They were still well represented and their selection problems certainly should not detract from England's outstanding performance.

We were seeking our first victory since 1972 and only our second since the inauguration of the competition in 1968.

Opposite: Crucial win for England's dynamic duo. Louis heads Briggs, Simmons and Mauger in the World Best Pairs final.

Above: Another couple of swells . . . Newcastle's brilliant brothers, Tom and Joe Owen. Joe has since joined Hull.

Even that solitary success in 1972 had been blanketed in controversy. England's Ray Wilson and Terry Betts had scored a total of 24 points, as had New Zealand's Ivan Mauger and Ronnie Moore. Wilson and Mauger had then faced each other in a tie-breaker, Mauger had fallen and Wilson ridden home alone.

A hollow victory? Perhaps. But there could be no arguments this time. Louis and Simmons, two of the most experienced and accomplished riders in England, aggregated 27 points to finish three ahead of Denmark and five ahead of Sweden.

Louis, the pride of Suffolk, British Champion in 1975, rode as brilliantly as he has ever done in international competition. Simmons, earlier crowned 1976 British Champion, was not quite as sharp at the gate as usual, but he battled for every point and the English pair knew their chances were good when they destroyed the Swedish challenge with a 5–1 in heat 10.

The only real threat came from Denmark, who had never previously won the Pairs title. Ole Olsen looked unbeatable and Finn Thomsen was doing enough to keep the Danes in the hunt. In fact, after four rides apiece they were in front.

The pendulum began to swing England's way when they scored a 5–1 against Australia, Simmons making a super-human effort to pass Phil Crump for the vital second place. And the Danes dropped points to Sweden.

But it was all on heat 20, when England faced the Danes. The superb Louis made no mistake. He rocketed away from the start and Olsen just could not catch him. Simmons was third and England were World Champions.

Louis recorded a paid maximum and Simmons ten points plus bonuses. Olsen and Thomson gave Denmark the runners-up spot and Sweden were third. Well out of the picture were New Zealand and their two great champions Ivan Mauger and Barry Briggs. Neither seemed to have the engine power to be competitive.

But it was a great English triumph and a smack in the eye for those who had insisted that Peter Collins should have been chosen. The selectors had stood by Louis and Simmons after their maximum points semi-final victory at Miskolc in Hungary.

However, it will be interesting to see what the selectors decide this year. For only the second time in the history of the competition, the final is being staged in England, at Belle Vue, Manchester, on 2 July. Belle Vue, is of course, Collins's home track and it seems unlikely that the new World Individual Champion will be overlooked.

It was at Belle Vue in 1974 that Collins and Dave Jessup, the favourites, flopped badly in the Pairs final and saw the title go to Sweden's Michanek and Soren Sjosten. What will happen there in '77? First it's up to the selectors and I wouldn't like to have their headache!

But, for the moment, let's savour our success at Eskilstuna and salute John Louis and Malcolm Simmons.

At home with the newly-weds

Only a few years ago Peter Collins was an apprentice fitter who could only dream of an expensive car and a lovely home. Now he has both.

The World Champion and his new wife Angela moved into this superb mock-Georgian mansion in Lymm, Cheshire, after their wedding last November.

Photographer *Wright Wood* dropped in at Christmas to snap these exclusive pictures.

'Nice of you to call,' say Peter and Angela.

Opposite above: Anyone for pheasant? Peter does the carving and Angela gets ready to serve up the croquette potatoes.

Opposite below: 'It makes a change to have you home,' says Angela as Peter tucks in.

Above: After lunch . . . a chance to relax and play a few records

. . . and to put the last few decorations on the Christmas tree.

Stars of tomorrow

Peter Collins *looks at young English riders who are on the brink of stardom.*

The best thing that ever happened to British Speedway, when it got back on its feet after the disastrous slump in the fifties and early sixties, was the formation of the British League's Second Division, in 1968.

Now they call it the National League but, when all's said and done, it is the Second Division. There is no slur intended because I have a lot to thank the Second Division for and I also believe it is the reason why England has such strength in depth these days.

Look at our full international team these days . . . John Louis, Dave Jessup, Gordon Kennett, Doug Wyer, Chris Morton, John Davis, myself . . . all products of the Second Division. Very few of today's top riders made it without a grounding in the 'feeder' league.

And a few more potential super stars are rolling off the assembly line, riders who will be looking to steal my thunder in the not too distant future.

Top of my list of Stars of Tomorrow is *Michael Lee*, the current British Junior Champion – a title I was lucky enough to win a few years ago.

Michael is only eighteen and has achieved a tremendous amount already. Having come this far it is now a question of whether he can push himself that bit further to reach the top.

I believe he has a better chance than anybody around at the moment. Thanks to his early success he has managed to rope in a few sponsors and his father, international moto-cross star Andy Lee, is behind him all the way. Michael has good equipment and is always immaculately prepared.

Some people say he is too tall and gangling but he copes very well and I don't think his height will be a hindrance. I expect big things from him this season after averaging nine points a meeting in the British League last year.

I will also be keeping my eye on *Joe Owen*, the twenty-year-old younger half of the famous Owen brothers from Ormskirk . . . and Newcastle!

Tom and Joe played major parts in the Newcastle Diamonds success story last season and the team's rejection by the British League promoters for 1977 must have come as a crushing blow to the brothers as well as the Tyneside fans.

Joe wanted to ride for Newcastle in the big League but now he has had to put his own career first and has joined Hull Vikings. Personally, I think he should have stepped up to the British League last season. He was far too good to stay in the 'Second Division', as he proved with his incredible success – Riders' Champion, No. 1 in the averages, Silver Helmet Match Race Champion for the entire season!

Joe has a very individual style of riding and I am sure he is going to do big things in the British League. It may take him a

KING'S
LYNN

Three gorgeous 'Penthouse Pets' bring a spot of glamour to the New National League Riders' Championship, won by Joe Owen (centre) from John Jackson (left) and Ted Hubbard.

season to 'feel' his way round some of the tracks but by next year I expect to see him established as one of the top English riders.

Now I'd like to move on to two brothers who are established in the British League and who are almost in the super star class . . . *Dave* and *Chris Morton.*

You will probably accuse me of bias because they have been friends of mine since junior school – and just as keen to win the World Championship.

I had something of a start on them but I expect them to catch me up in the next couple of years. Dave is, in fact, a few months older than me but he didn't get going as a rider until a year after me. Now he is firmly established as Hackney's No. 1 and he had a great season last year. He is a more stylish rider than Chris, sitting very upright on his bike.

Michael Lee, reigning British Junior Champion and tipped for the top by Peter Collins.

Chris is twenty and relies more on balance. Since he got into the Belle Vue team, hundreds of people have compared his style with the late Peter Craven and I can certainly see similarities. Chris has made terrific progress, since he got him-

The other Morton brother, Dave, had a great season in 1976 and represented Hackney in the British League Riders' Championship. He is pictured here with Reading's No. 1 Dave Jessup.

self some decent equipment, and it was a tremendous achievement to reach the World final last season.

He has given me a few roastings at Belle Vue, too, so I will have to look out for him this season. I suggest you do, too, because he is a great prospect.

Of the riders who are up and coming in the National League, I rate *Steve Lawson* very strongly. This nineteen-year-old from Workington was signed by Belle Vue last season and I was very impressed with his style and form until an injury knocked him back.

Steve has made remarkable progress because he did not make his League debut until 1974. Clearly the experience he gained in cycle Speedway and riding motor bikes on the sands, has helped him considerably.

Brilliant Belle Vue star Chris Morton snatches a drink between races.

Looking through the National League I can see several riders with potential . . . like Eastbourne's *Steve Weatherley*, Boston's *Rob Hollingworth*, Ellesmere Port's *Chris Turner* – another rider recruited by Belle Vue for 1977 – not to mention my own kid brothers *Les* and *Phil Collins*.

You can be sure that, as long as there is a 'Second Division' or National League England's future as a Speedway nation will remain very rosy.

What's new in 1977

Richard Bott *previews the new season with a look at some of the major decisions taken by the promoters at their close-season conferences and how they will affect Speedway in '77.*

Rider control, guest riders and noise were the three big talking points at the January conference of British League promoters in Malta. And not before time. The first two have long been an embarrassment to Speedway and its acceptance by the cynics, the third has always been a threat to the sport's future.

Rider control is the 'rob Peter to pay Paul' policy to balance team strengths and it was a sound enough idea a decade ago, when the British League was struggling for a foothold.

But in recent years it has been a source of amusement to outsiders, who have scoffed at the way a successful team are penalized by having a top rider allocated elsewhere. That, together with the wilful misuse of the guest rider system, has brought the sport more bad publicity than it can afford.

Now, at last, common sense prevails. Rider control still exists but in a much more acceptable form. Ambitious promoters need no longer live in fear of building a successful team only to see it carved up the following season for the sake of other promoters who are no better than parasites.

The promoters have appointed a rider control sub-committee to act as 'watch dogs'. This committee will act in an advisory capacity but will have no responsibility for re-allocating riders.

Promoters are free to negotiate transfers and to encourage and train new talent.

But, under the new scheme, there is a yardstick. Teams must not start the season with an aggregate calculated match average of more than 52 points. Only when a team exceeds that maximum will they be subject to rider control. The new legislation also includes the mandate that no team may introduce a rider or riders, other than their own juniors, if such introduction would take the team's total average above 48 points.

Guest riders have long been a bone of contention with me and I applaud the efforts of one promoter to have them abolished. The motion was defeated but only by a very small majority, an indication that the guest rider 'joke' is wearing thin with more and more promoters.

There is to be a tightening up on the use of guests in 1977 and that, at least, is a step in the right direction – if it is enforced.

Now for the noise factor. Anyone who has ever been to a Speedway meeting will appreciate that noise is not only prevalent but an essential part of the fun and atmosphere. However, people tend to live within the precincts of Speedway stadiums and many of them object to the roar of 500 c.c. engines. In fact, these objections are invariably raised whenever

Richard Greer (right), seen here chasing Halifax's Chris Pusey, switches from White City to Birmingham this season.

a promoter attempts to open a new venue.

Planning permission has been refused on countless occasions because of the noise factor, and existing tracks have been forced to close.

Last season a form of silencer was introduced which did not meet with the overall approval of the riders. Some claimed the silencer improved the performance of their engines, others that it had a detrimental effect. Now a silencer is being introduced, designed specifically for Speedway by research scientists at Manchester University. Engine design will be affected in the future as more stringent regulations for noise abatement are brought in. And promoters are having to consider other ways of controlling noise, such as building noise baffle walls at their stadiums.

The promoters in the past, have been accused of burying their heads in the sand. Now they have taken positive steps not only to safeguard the future of the sport but also to give its existing image a face-lift.

What else is new in '77? Well, excitement is mounting in the West Country because Bristol are back after an absence of seventeen years. The patient fans who kept the old Bristol Bulldogs Supporters Club going for nearly two decades have now been rewarded and there will be British League Speedway at Eastville Stadium, home of Bristol Rovers FC, this season.

Bristol's gain is Newport's loss because Newport's British League licence has been transferred to Bristol.

Among the close-season transfer deals are . . . Belle Vue's Paul Tyrer to King's Lynn and Geoff Pusey to Wolverhampton . . . Birmingham's Soren Sjosten to Wolverhampton . . . Richard Greer from White City to Birmingham . . . Bob Valentine from Birmingham to Cradley United . . . Kevin Holden from Exeter to Poole.

Cradley also came up with the scoop signing of the close season when they persuaded former World Champion Anders Michanek to return to British Speedway.

Belle Vue promoter Jack Fearnley is the new supremo of the British League, elected chairman in succession to Reg Fearman. Ipswich promoter John Berry has joined the management committee.

Charles Foot, doyen of British promoters and long-serving member of the management committee, has become the first president of the Promoter's Association.

And the New National League has dropped the 'new' to become the National League.

The National League welcomes the return of Edinburgh, the addition of Newport and the birth of a new competition . . . the Grand National.

It's all 'new' in '77!

Spot the Team

How good are you at recognizing race jackets? Take a look at the following and see how many you can get right. The answers are on page 112.

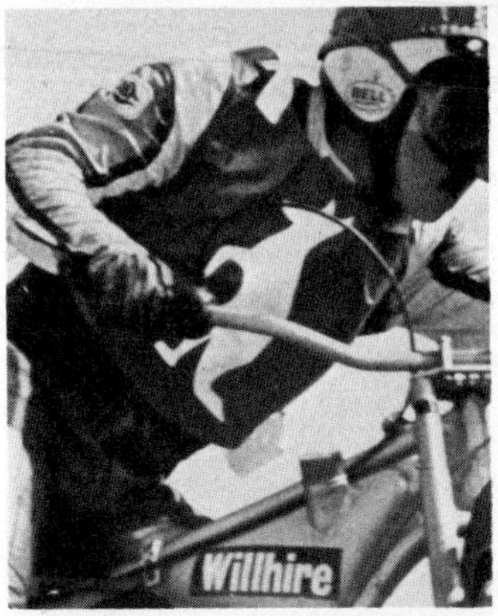

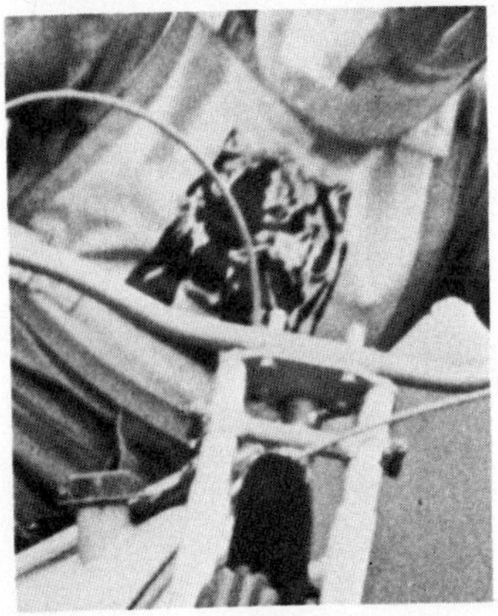

International results 1976

World Team Cup Final
White City, London, 19 September

Australia 31 (P. Crump 11, B. Sanders 7, P. Herne 7, J. Boulger 6)
Poland 28 (E. Jancarz 9, M. Cieslak 7, Z. Plech 6, J. Rembas 5, B. Proch 1)
Sweden 26 (A. Michanek 11, B. Persson 8, L. Andersson 5, B. Jansson 1, C. Lofqvist 1)
Russia 11 (Valeri Gordeev 5, V. Paznikov 2, Vladimir Gordeev 2, G. Chlinovski 2, V. Trofimov 0)

World Best Pairs Final
Eskilstuna, Sweden, 17 June

England 27 (J. Louis 17, M. Simmons 10)
Denmark 24 (O. Olsen 16, F. Thomsen 8)
Sweden 22 (B. Persson 11, B. Jansson 11)
Australia 16 (P. Crump 10, B. Sanders 6)
New Zealand 15 (I. Mauger 8, B. Briggs 7)
Scotland 12 (J. McMillan 10, G. Hunter 2)
Poland 10 (E. Jancarz 7, Z. Plech 3)

England v. Rest of the World
Vojns, Denmark, 15 July

England 41 (P. Collins 14, G. Kennett 7, M. Simmons 6, M. Ashby 4, D. Jessup 4, J. Davis 3, D. Morton 3)
Rest of the World 43 (O. Olsen 12, A. Michanek 7, I. Mauger 7, B. Briggs 5, E. Muller 5, P. Crump 5, J. Stancl 2)

Polish tour of Britain 1976

16 April	Newport 60, Poland 17
19 April	King's Lynn 54, Poland 24
21 April	Poole 43, Poland 34
23 April	Hackney 45, Poland 33
24 April	Halifax 46, Poland 32
28 April	Coventry 52, Poland 26

USSR tour of Britain 1976

4 June	Wolverhampton 56, USSR 22
7 June	Reading 46, USSR 32
9 June	Belle Vue 53, USSR 25
10 June	Sheffield 51, USSR 27
12 June	Swindon 47, USSR 31
14 June	Exeter 53, USSR 25

England v. Australasia
Newcastle, 9 August

England 77 (J. Owen 18, J. Jackson 18, L. Collins 14, T. Owen 13, R. Hollingworth 8, C. Turner 6)
Australasia 30 (C. Farquharson 8, P. Michelides 6, R. Wright 6, E. Argall 3, R. Blackadder 3, M. McKeon 2, A. Cowan 1, R. Adlington 1)

Workington, 13 August

England 66 (S. Lawson 18, L. Collins 13, J. Owen 11, B. Havelock 10, C. Goad 7, T. Owen 6, G. Jones 1)
Australasia 42 (L. Sansom 12, R. Wright 7, P. Michelides 7, D. Gifford 5, M. McKeon 5, S. Mountford 4, C. Farquharson 2, E. Argall 0)

Scunthorpe, 16 August

England 44 (S. Lawson 16, K. Evans 14, L. Collins 7, T. Featherstone 4, R. Hollingworth 2, A. Hines 1, P, Kynman 0, B. Havelock 0)
Australasia 63 (B. Cribb 18, D. Underwood 11, C. Farquharson 9, P. Bass 9, C. Askew 8, R. Adlington 6, S. Mountford 2, M. McKeon 0)

Teesside, 19 August

England 60 (T. Owen 17, J. Owen 17, S. Wilcock 11, T. Leadbitter 5, R. Hollingworth 4, P. Smith 4, J. Jackson 2, A. Cusworth 0)
Australasia 48 (B. Cribb 15, D. Underwood 14, B. Humphreys 12, P. Michelides 4, M. McKeon 1, A. Cowan 1, S. Mountford 1, R. Blackadder 0)

Boston, 22 August

England 65 (J. Owen 16, K. Evans 16, T. Owen 14, T. Featherstone 10, R. Hollingworth 7, M. Yeates 1, S. Cope 1, K. Matthews 0)
Australasia 43 (B. Humphreys 13, J. Titman 11, D. Underwood 10, P. Bass 4, P. Michelides 2, R. Adlington 2, C. Askew 1, R. Blackadder 0)

Ellesmere Port, 24 August

England 80 (J. Owen 18, J. Jackson 17, T. Owen 14, L. Collins 12, S. Lawson 10, C. Turner 9)
Australasia 28 (B. Cribb 10, B. Humphreys 8, P. Bass 7, R. Adlington 3, S. Mountford 0, M. McKeon 0, C. Askew 0, M. Fullerton 0)

Stoke, 26 August

England 63 (J. Owen 16, L. Collins 15, S. Finch 11, T. Owen 10, K. Evans 7, M. Shakespeare 4, M. Newton 0)
Australasia 45 (M. Shirra 15, D. Underwood 12, R. Day 10, P. Bass 6, P. Michelides 2, J. Titman 0, R. Adlington 0)

Canterbury, 28 August

England 60 (J. Owen 15, T. Hubbard 14, S. Weatherley 12, L. Rumsey 8, H. Saunders 6, G. Clifton 4, B. Kennett 1, M. Yeates 0)
Australasia 48 (P. Herne 15, J. Titman 10, S. Koppe 7, P. Bass 6, B. Spelta 4, D. Kennady 2, B. Sanders 2, T. Casserly 2)

England won the series 7–1

ʹTop Tenʹ

1976 National Averages

Gulf British League

	Matches	Rides	Points	Bonus points	Total points	Calculated match averages
1 JOHN LOUIS (*Ipswich*)	28	116	315	7	322	11.10
2 Ivan Mauger (*Exeter*)	32	136	368	6	374	11.00
3 Ole Olsen (*Coventry*)	31	136	360	14	374	11.00
4 Peter Collins (*Belle Vue*)	34	141	379	8	387	10.98
5 Phil Crump (*Newport*)	35	164	434	4	438	10.69
6 Dave Jessup (*Reading*)	36	152	385	11	396	10.42
7 Malcolm Simmons (*Poole*)	34	158	399	8	407	10.30
8 Dave Morton (*Hackney*)	32	137	346	6	352	10.28
9 John Boulger (*Cradley*)	33	145	355	5	360	9.93
10 Martin Ashby (*Swindon*)	36	159	374	19	393	9.89

New National League

	Matches	Rides	Points	Bonus points	Total points	Calculated match averages
1 JOE OWEN (*Newcastle*)	31	133	384	0	384	11.55
2 Tom Owen (*Newcastle*)	34	144	343	27	370	10.28
3 Steve Weatherley (*Eastbourne*)	30	134	336	8	344	10.27
4 John Jackson (*Ellesmere Port*)	33	142	356	6	362	10.20
5 Laurie Etheridge (*Crayford*)	33	145	342	19	361	9.96
6 Brian Clark (*Peterborough*)	28	114	261	17	278	9.75
7 Rob Hollingworth (*Boston*)	34	157	373	7	380	9.68
8 Chris Turner (*Ellesmere Port*)	27	113	259	11	270	9.56
9 Les Collins (*Stoke*)	33	154	349	15	364	9.45
10 Ted Hubbard (*Rye House*)	32	141	314	12	326	9.25

Figures compiled by official BSPA statistician Bryan Seery

How your team finished

Final tables 1976

Gulf British League

	Home P	W	D	L	Race points For Against	Away W	D	L	Race points For Against	Match points
1 IPSWICH	36	18	0	0	853–550	9	1	8	702–702	55
2 Belle Vue	36	15	1	2	833–570	8	1	9	682–719	48
3 Exeter	36	18	0	0	792–607	5	2	11	668–731	48
4 Coventry	36	18	0	0	829½–573½	3	2	13	616½–784½	44
5 Swindon	36	15	3	0	828–574	4	1	13	634–769	42
6 Reading	36	14	2	2	795–609	5	1	12	682–716	41
7 Hackney	36	16	0	2	761–636	4	0	14	631–768	40
8 Newport	36	18	0	0	841½–559½	1	1	16	595–807	39
9 Cradley	36	16	1	1	772–631	3	0	15	625–777	39
10 Poole	36	15	0	3	808–593	3	1	14	583–819	37
11 Wolverhampton	36	12	0	6	738–663	6	1	11	609–793	37
12 Hull	36	14	0	4	797–602	4	0	14	672½–729½	36
13 White City	36	13	1	4	794½–609½	3	2	13	643–758	35
14 King's Lynn	36	14	2	2	798–602	2	1	15	628–773	35
15 Halifax	36	14	1	3	771½–630½	0	0	18	533–870	29
16 Wimbledon	36	11	2	5	756–645	1	1	16	604½–798½	27
17 Sheffield	36	13	1	4	745–658	0	0	18	576–825	27
18 Birmingham	36	7	0	11	658–741	0	0	18	538½–862½	14
19 Leicester	36	5	1	12	683–719	0	0	18	550–852	11

New National League

	Home P	W	D	L	Race points For Against	Away W	D	L	Race points For Against	Match points
1 NEWCASTLE	34	17	0	0	906–419	13	1	3	736–588	61
2 Ellesmere Port	34	16	1	0	830½–492½	8	0	9	616–704	49
3 Workington	34	16	0	1	818–505	4	1	12	587½–730½	41
4 Canterbury	34	15	0	2	815–507	5	0	12	529–795	40
5 Rye House	34	14	1	2	818½–500½	3	1	13	539–705	36
6 Crayford	34	15	1	1	810–508	2	0	15	544–778	35
7 Coatbridge	34	15	0	2	795–522	2	1	14	521–798	35
8 Eastbourne	34	16	0	1	836–484	1	0	16	525–797	34
9 Peterborough	34	14	1	2	745–501	2	1	14	566–759	34
10 Berwick	34	16	0	1	772–548	1	0	16	506–812	34
11 Stoke	34	14	0	3	736–588	1	1	15	568–752	31
12 Boston	34	14	1	2	749–573	1	0	16	549–772	31
13 Mildenhall	34	14	0	3	746–578	1	1	15	524–800	31
14 Oxford	34	14	1	2	760–564	0	0	17	497–746	29
15 Weymouth	34	10	1	6	709–611	1	1	15	477½–843½	24
16 Paisley	34	12	0	5	723–598	0	0	17	429–894	24
17 Scunthorpe	34	10	1	6	678–564	1	0	16	506–815	23
18 Teesside	34	10	0	7	690–630	0	0	17	473–848	20

Parade of the Champions

FIM CHAMPIONSHIP OF THE WORLD

Year	Place	Rider
1936	1	Lionel Van Praag (*Australia*)
	2	Eric Langton (*England*)
	3	'Bluey' Wilkinson (*Australia*)
1937	1	Jack Milne (*USA*)
	2	Wilbur Lamoreaux (*USA*)
	3	Cordy Milne (*USA*)
1938	1	'Bluey' Wilkinson (*Australia*)
	2	Jack Milne (*USA*)
	3	Wilbur Lamoreaux (*USA*)
1949	1	Tommy Price (*England*)
	2	Jack Parker (*England*)
	3	Louis Lawson (*England*)
1950	1	Freddie Williams (*Wales*)
	2	Wally Green (*England*)
	3	Graham Warren (*Australia*)
1951	1	Jack Young (*Australia*)
	2	Split Waterman (*England*)
	3	Jack Biggs (*Australia*)
1952	1	Jack Young (*Australia*)
	2	Freddie Williams (*Wales*)
	3	Bob Oakley (*England*)
1953	1	Freddie Williams (*Wales*)
	2	Split Waterman (*England*)
	3	Geoff Mardon (*New Zealand*)
1954	1	Ronnie Moore (*New Zealand*)
	2	Brian Crutcher (*England*)
	3	Olle Nygren (*Sweden*)
1955	1	Peter Craven (*England*)
	2	Ronnie Moore (*New Zealand*)
	3	Barry Briggs (*New Zealand*)
1956	1	Ove Fundin (*Sweden*)
	2	Ronnie Moore (*New Zealand*)
	3	Arthur Forrest (*England*)
1957	1	Barry Briggs (*New Zealand*)
	2	Ove Fundin (*Sweden*)
	3	Peter Craven (*England*)
1958	1	Barry Briggs (*New Zealand*)
	2	Ove Fundin (*Sweden*)
	3	Aub Lawson (*Australia*)
1959	1	Ronnie Moore (*New Zealand*)
	3	Ove Fundin (*Sweden*)
	3	Barry Briggs (*New Zealand*)
1960	1	Ove Fundin (*Sweden*)
	2	Ronnie Moore (*New Zealand*)
	3	Peter Craven (*England*)
1961	1	Ove Fundin (*Sweden*)
	2	Bjorn Knutsson (*Sweden*)
	3	Gote Nordin (*Sweden*)
1962	1	Peter Craven (*England*)
	2	Barry Briggs (*New Zealand*)
	3	Ove Fundin (*Sweden*)
1963	1	Ove Fundin (*Sweden*)
	2	Bjorn Knutsson (*Sweden*)
	3	Barry Briggs (*New Zealand*)
1964	1	Barry Briggs (*New Zealand*)
	2	Igor Plechanov (*USSR*)
	3	Ove Fundin (*Sweden*)
1965	1	Bjorn Knutsson (*Sweden*)
	2	Igor Plechanov (*USSR*)
	3	Ove Fundin (*Sweden*)
1966	1	Barry Briggs (*New Zealand*)
	2	Sverre Harrfeldt (*Norway*)
	3	Antoni Woryna (*Poland*)
1967	1	Ove Fundin (*Sweden*)
	2	Bengt Jansson (*Sweden*)
	3	Ivan Mauger (*New Zealand*)
1968	1	Ivan Mauger (*New Zealand*)
	2	Barry Briggs (*New Zealand*)
	3	Edward Jancarz (*Poland*)
1969	1	Ivan Mauger (*New Zealand*)
	2	Barry Briggs (*New Zealand*)
	3	Soren Sjosten (*Sweden*)
1970	1	Ivan Mauger (*New Zealand*)
	2	Pawel Waloszek (*Poland*)
	3	Antoni Woryna (*Poland*)
1971	1	Ole Olsen (*Denmark*)
	2	Ivan Mauger (*New Zealand*)
	3	Bengt Jansson (*Sweden*)

1972 1 Ivan Mauger (*New Zealand*)
2 Bernt Persson (*Sweden*)
3 Ole Olsen (*Denmark*)

1973 1 Jerzy Szczakiel (*Poland*)
2 Ivan Mauger (*New Zealand*)
3 Zenon Plech (*Poland*)

1974 1 Anders Michanek (*Sweden*)
2 Ivan Mauger (*New Zealand*)
3 Soren Sjosten (*Sweden*)

1975 1 Ole Olsen (*Denmark*)
2 Anders Michanek (*Sweden*)
3 John Louis (*England*)

1976 1 Peter Collins (*England*)
2 Malcolm Simmons (*England*)
3 Phil Crump (*Australia*)

WORLD TEAM CUP

1960 (*Gothenburg*)	Sweden 44, England 30, Czechoslovakia 15, Poland 7
1961 (*Wroclaw*)	Poland 32, Sweden 31, England 21, Czechoslovakia 12
1962 (*Slany*)	Sweden 36, Great Britain 24, Poland 20, Czechoslovakia 16
1963 (*Vienna*)	Sweden 37, Czechoslovakia 27, Great Britain 25, Poland 7
1964 (*Abensburg*)	Sweden 34, USSR 25, Great Britain 21, Poland 16
1965 (*Kempten*)	Poland 38, Sweden 33, Great Britain 18, USSR 7
1966 (*Wroclaw*)	Poland 40, USSR 26, Sweden 22, Great Britain 8
1967 (*Malmo*)	Sweden 32, Poland 26, Great Britain 19, USSR 10
1968 (*London*)	Great Britain 40, Sweden 30, Poland 19, Czechoslovakia 7
1969 (*Rybnik*)	Poland 31, Great Britain 27, USSR 23, Sweden 12
1970 (*London*)	Sweden 41, Great Britain 31, Poland 18, Czechoslovakia 3
1971 (*Wroclaw*)	Great Britain 37, USSR 22, Poland 19, Sweden 18
1972 (*Olching*)	Great Britain 36, USSR 21, Poland 21, Sweden 18
1973 (*London*)	Great Britain 37, Sweden 31, USSR 20, Poland 8
1974 (*Katowice*)	Great Britain 42, Sweden 31, Poland 13, USSR 10
1975 (*Norden*)	England 41, USSR 29, Sweden 17, Poland 9
1976 (*London*)	Australia 31, Poland 28, Sweden 26, USSR 11

WORLD BEST PAIRS CHAMPIONS

1968 Sweden (O. Fundin and T. Harrysson)
1969 New Zealand (I. Mauger and B. Andrews)
1970 New Zealand (I. Mauger and R. Moore)
1971 Poland (J. Szczakiel and A. Wyglenda)
1972 England (R. Wilson and T. Betts)
1973 Sweden (A. Michanek and T. Jansson)
1974 Sweden (A. Michanek and S. Sjosten)
1975 Sweden (A. Michanek and T. Jansson)
1976 England (J. Louis and M. Simmons)

BRITISH LEAGUE RIDERS' CHAMPIONS

at Belle Vue, Manchester

1965 Barry Briggs (*Swindon*)
1966 Barry Briggs (*Swindon*)
1967 Barry Briggs (*Swindon*)
1968 Barry Briggs (*Swindon*)
1969 Barry Briggs (*Swindon*)
1970 Barry Briggs (*Swindon*)
1971 Ivan Mauger (*Belle Vue*)
1972 Ole Olsen (*Wolverhampton*)
1973 Ivan Mauger (*Exeter*)
1974 Peter Collins (*Belle Vue*)
1975 Peter Collins (*Belle Vue*)
1976 Ole Olsen (*Coventry*)

BRITISH LEAGUE CHAMPIONS

First Division

1965 West Ham
1966 Halifax
1967 Swindon
1968 Coventry
1969 Poole
1970 Belle Vue
1971 Belle Vue
1972 Belle Vue
1973 Reading
1974 Exeter
1975 Ipswich
1976 Ipswich

Second Division

1968 Belle Vue 'B'
1969 Belle Vue 'B'
1970 Canterbury
1971 Eastbourne
1972 Crewe
1973 Boston
1974 Birmingham

NEW NATIONAL LEAGUE CHAMPIONS

1975 Birmingham
1976 Newcastle

NEW NATIONAL LEAGUE RIDERS' CHAMPIONS

at Wimbledon

1975 Laurie Etheridge (*Crayford*)
1976 Joe Owen (*Newcastle*)

BRITISH LEAGUE KNOCK-OUT

Division One

1965 West Ham
1966 Halifax
1967 Coventry
1968 Wimbledon
1969 Wimbledon
1970 Wimbledon
1971 Hackney
1972 Belle Vue
1973 Belle Vue
1974 Sheffield
1975 Belle Vue
1976 Ipswich

Division Two

1968 Canterbury
1969 Belle Vue 'B'
1970 Ipswich
1971 Ipswich
1972 Crewe
1973 Boston
1974 Birmingham

SECOND DIVISION RIDERS' CHAMPIONS

at Hackney

1968 Graham Plant (*Middlesbrough*)
1969 Geoff Ambrose (*Crayford*)
1970 Dave Jessup (*Eastbourne*)
1971 John Louis (*Ipswich*)

at Wimbledon

1972 Phil Crump (*Crewe*)
1973 Arthur Price (*Boston*)
1974 Carl Glover (*Boston*)

NEW NATIONAL LEAGUE KNOCK-OUT CUP

1975 Eastbourne
1976 Newcastle

INTER-DIVISIONAL KNOCK-OUT CUP

1975 Belle Vue
1976 Hull

CONTINENTAL CHAMPIONS

1965 Andrzej Wyglenda (*Poland*)
1966 Andrzej Pogorzelski (*Poland*)
1967 Andrzej Wyglenda (*Poland*)
1968 Gennady Kurilenko (*USSR*)
1969 Antoni Woryna (*Poland*)
1970 Hans Jurgen Fritz (*East Germany*)
1971 Henryk Glucklich (*Poland*)
1972 Victor Trofimov (*USSR*)
1973 Valeri Gordeev (*USSR*)
1974 Vladimir Gordeev (*USSR*)
1975 Edward Jancarz (*Poland*)
1976 Egon Muller (*West Germany*)

RUSSIAN CHAMPIONS

1965 Igor Plechanov
1966 Farid Szajnurov
1967 Victor Trofimov
1968 Igor Plechanov
1969 Valeri Klementiev
1970 Vladimir Gordeev
1971 Vladimir Gordeev
1972 Vladimir Gordeev
1973 Vladimir Gordeev
1974 Vladimir Gordeev
1975 Valeri Gordeev
1976 Valeri Gordeev

BRITISH CHAMPIONS

1965 Barry Briggs
1966 Barry Briggs
1967 Barry Briggs
1968 Ivan Mauger
1969 Barry Briggs
1970 Ivan Mauger
1971 Ivan Mauger
1972 Ivan Mauger
1973 Ray Wilson
1974 Eric Boocock
1975 John Louis
1976 Malcolm Simmons

SWEDISH CHAMPIONS

1965 Gote Nordin
1966 Ove Fundin
1967 Ove Fundin
1968 Leif Enecrona
1969 Ove Fundin
1970 Ove Fundin
1971 Gote Nordin
1972 Anders Michanek
1973 Tommy Johanneson
1974 Tommy Jansson
1975 Anders Michanek
1976 Anders Michanek

EUROPEAN CHAMPIONS

1965 Ove Fundin (*Sweden*)
1966 Ivan Mauger (*New Zealand*)
1967 Andrzej Wyglenda (*Poland*)
1968 Pawel Waloszek (*Poland*)
1969 Valeri Klementiev (*USSR*)
1970 Ivan Mauger (*New Zealand*)
1971 Ivan Mauger (*New Zealand*)
1972 Pawel Waloszek (*Poland*)
1973 Anders Michanek (*Sweden*)
1974 Peter Collins (*England*)
1975 Ivan Mauger (*New Zealand*)
1976 *No competition*

POLISH CHAMPIONS

1965 Stanislav Tkocz
1966 Antoni Woryna
1967 Zygmunt Pytko
1968 Andrzej Wyglenda
1969 Andrzej Wyglenda
1970 Edmund Migos
1971 Jerzy Gryt
1972 Zenon Plech
1973 Andrzej Wyglenda
1974 Zenon Plech
1975 Edward Jancarz
1976 Zdislaw Dobrucki

What Peter Collins won in 1976

16 April	John Player No. 6 Classic, Belle Vue
3 May	World Championship qualifying round, Birmingham
7 May	The Olympique, Wolverhampton
19 May	World Championship semi-final, White City
17 June	Yorkshire Bank Trophy, Sheffield
26 June	World Championship Intercontinental final, Wembley
4 August	*Daily Mirror* Grand Prix final, White City
11 August	Silver Plume, Swindon
5 September	WORLD CHAMPIONSHIP FINAL, Katowice
7 September	Golden Gauntlets, Leicester
20 September	Manpower Championship, Reading
30 October	Pride of the East, King's Lynn

World Championship diary 1977

19 February	Australasian Final, Sydney
14 May	British quarter-final, Reading
16 May	British quarter-final, Cradley
18 May	British quarter-final, King's Lynn
20 May	British quarter-final, Hackney
29 May	Continental semi-final, Krsko, Yugoslavia
29 May	Continental semi-final, Norden, West Germany
29 May	Nordic Final, Tampere, Finland
19 June	World Team Cup U K qualifying round, Ipswich
25 June	Continental Final, Togliatti, USSR
27 June	British semi-final, Birmingham
29 June	British semi-final, Poole
2 July	WORLD BEST PAIRS FINAL, Belle Vue
13 July	British Final, Coventry
21 August	Inter-continental final, White City
2 September	WORLD INDIVIDUAL FINAL, Gothenburg, Sweden
11 September	WORLD LONG-TRACK FINAL, Aalborg, Denmark
18 September	WORLD TEAM CUP FINAL, Wroclaw, Poland

Other important dates

24 March	*Daily Express* Spring Classic, Wimbledon
4 June	National League Best Pairs Championship, Belle Vue
6 June	Embassy Internationale, Wimbledon
7 August	National League Four-team tourney, Peterborough
24 September	National League Riders' Championship, Wimbledon
29 September	British League Best Pairs Championship, Ipswich
5 October	British League Riders' Championship, Belle Vue
15 October	*Daily Mirror* Grand Prix Final, White City

Spot the Team - Answers

A
Hackney Hawks

B
Ipswich Witches

C
Australia

D
Peterborough Panthers

E
Swindon Robins

F
Coatbridge Tigers

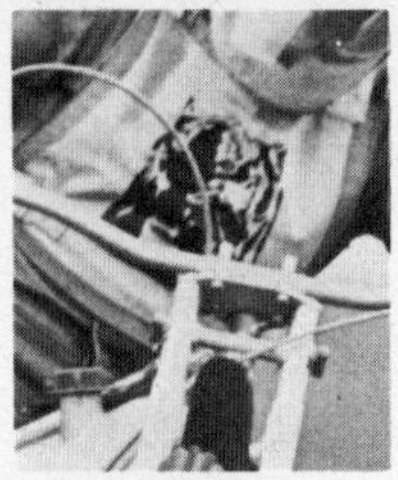

G
Sheffield Tigers

H
Reading Racers

I
Coventry Bees